First World War
and Army of Occupation
War Diary
France, Belgium and Germany

14 DIVISION
43 Infantry Brigade
Duke of Cambridge's Own (Middlesex Regiment)
20th Battalion
1 June 1918 - 18 June 1919

WO95/1910/3

The Naval & Military Press Ltd
www.nmarchive.com
Published in association with The National Archives

Published by

The Naval & Military Press Ltd

Unit 10 Ridgewood Industrial Park,

Uckfield, East Sussex,

TN22 5QE England

Tel: +44 (0) 1825 749494

www.naval-military-press.com

www.nmarchive.com

This diary has been reprinted in facsimile from the original. Any imperfections are inevitably reproduced and the quality may fall short of modern type and cartographic standards.

© **Crown Copyright**
Images reproduced by permission of The National Archives, London, England, 2015.

Contents

Document type	Place/Title	Date From	Date To
Heading	WO95/1910 14 Div-43 Inf Bde 20 Middx Regt Jun 1918-Jun 1919		
Heading	14th Division 43rd Infy Bde 20th Bn Middx Regt Jun 1918-Jun 1919 From 40 Div 121 Bde		
Heading	20th (S) Battalion Middlesex Regt. War Diary June 1918. Vol 23		
War Diary	Desvres	01/06/1918	16/06/1918
War Diary	Boulogne	17/06/1918	17/06/1918
War Diary	England	17/06/1918	17/06/1918
War Diary	Brookwood	17/06/1918	17/06/1918
War Diary	Bullswater Camp.	17/06/1918	18/06/1918
War Diary	Bullswater	18/06/1918	20/06/1918
War Diary	Bullswater Camp	21/06/1918	30/06/1918
Heading	War Diary 20th Batty Middlesex Regiment. July 1918.		
War Diary	Bullswater Camp.	01/07/1918	04/07/1918
War Diary	Folkestone	05/07/1918	05/07/1918
War Diary	Bologne	06/07/1918	06/07/1918
War Diary	Boursin	07/07/1918	10/07/1918
War Diary	Licques Area	11/07/1918	11/07/1918
War Diary	Harbinghem	12/07/1918	12/07/1918
War Diary	Noardausques.	13/07/1918	13/07/1918
War Diary	Zudrove	14/07/1918	15/07/1918
War Diary	Terdeghem	16/07/1918	28/07/1918
War Diary	Terdeghem Broxeele	29/07/1918	29/07/1918
War Diary	Broxeele-Le-Marais.	30/07/1918	30/07/1918
War Diary	Lemarais-Nortleulinghem	31/07/1918	31/07/1918
Operation(al) Order(s)	20th Battalion, Middlesex Regiment. Operation Order No: 1. A	02/07/1918	02/07/1918
Operation(al) Order(s)	20th Battalion, Middlesex Regiment. Operation Order No: 2.	02/07/1918	02/07/1918
Miscellaneous	Nominal Roll Of Officers Proceeding Overseas B1		
Miscellaneous	Honours & Awards Gained By The 20th (S) Battalion Middlesex Regt. In The King's Birthday Honours Gazette 1918. C		
Miscellaneous	To:- O.C. "A" Company, "B" Company, "C" Company, "D" Company, Transport Officer	10/07/1918	10/07/1918
Operation(al) Order(s)	20th Battalion, Middlesex Regiment. Operation Order No. 3.	10/07/1918	10/07/1918
Operation(al) Order(s)	20th Battalion, Middlesex Regiment. Operation Order No: 4.	11/07/1918	11/07/1918
Operation(al) Order(s)	20th Battalion, Middlesex Regiment. Operation Order No: 5.	12/07/1918	12/07/1918
Operation(al) Order(s)	20th Battalion, Middlesex Regiment. Operation Order No: 6.	14/07/1918	14/07/1918
Miscellaneous	20th Battalion, The Middlesex Regiment.	22/07/1918	22/07/1918
Miscellaneous	20th Battalion Middlesex Regiment.	22/07/1918	22/07/1918
Operation(al) Order(s)	20th Battalion, Middlesex Regiment. Operation Order No: 7.	28/07/1918	28/07/1918
Miscellaneous	March Table.		

Type	Description	Date From	Date To
Operation(al) Order(s)	Administrative Arrangements. To Operation Order, No: 7.	28/07/1918	28/07/1918
Operation(al) Order(s)	Administrative Order No 2 To Operation Order No 7	29/07/1918	29/07/1918
Operation(al) Order(s)	Administrative Order No 3. To Operation Orders No 7	30/07/1918	30/07/1918
Miscellaneous	Distribution		
Heading	Vol 25 War Diary 20th Battalion Middlesex Regiment August 1918.		
Miscellaneous			
Miscellaneous	Nortleulinghem	01/08/1918	12/08/1918
War Diary	Lesmarais	12/08/1918	12/08/1918
War Diary	Broxeele	13/08/1918	14/08/1918
War Diary	Esquelbecq	15/08/1918	15/08/1918
War Diary	Droglandt.	15/08/1918	17/08/1918
War Diary	Proven	17/08/1918	18/08/1918
War Diary	Siege Camp.	18/08/1918	19/08/1918
War Diary	Right Brigade Sector Ypres	19/08/1918	23/08/1918
War Diary	Right Brigade Sector	23/08/1918	24/08/1918
War Diary	Orillia Camp.	24/08/1918	28/08/1918
War Diary	Support.	28/08/1918	28/08/1918
War Diary	Right Brigade Sector. Ypres Front	28/08/1918	29/08/1918
War Diary	Support Camp	29/08/1918	31/08/1918
War Diary	Ypres Front Support	31/08/1918	31/08/1918
Miscellaneous	In the Inter-Platoon Competition. The Following were the marks awarded:- A		
Miscellaneous	Supplementary Orders to Routine Orders Issue No: 28 d/5-8-18.	05/08/1918	05/08/1918
Operation(al) Order(s)	20th Battalion, Middlesex Regiment. Operation Order No. 10.	11/08/1918	11/08/1918
Operation(al) Order(s)	20th Bn Middlesex Regt. No 12 Operation Order No 11.	12/08/1918	12/08/1918
Operation(al) Order(s)	20th Battalion, Middlesex Regiment. Operation Order No. 12.	13/08/1918	13/08/1918
Miscellaneous	20th Battalion, Middlesex Regiment. Operation Order No. 13.	14/08/1918	14/08/1918
Operation(al) Order(s)	20th Battalion, Middlesex Regiment. Operation Order No. 14 C4	16/08/1918	16/08/1918
Operation(al) Order(s)	20th Battalion, Middlesex Regiment. Operation Order No. 15 C5	17/08/1918	17/08/1918
Miscellaneous	Warning Order and Administrative Orders.		
Operation(al) Order(s)	20th Battalion Middlesex Regiment. Operation Order No. 16.	19/08/1918	19/08/1918
Miscellaneous	20th Middlesex Regiment. Right Brigade Sector. Provisional Defence Scheme.		
Miscellaneous	Provisional Defence Scheme Right Brigade Sector	13/08/1918	13/08/1918
Miscellaneous	F To Come		
Operation(al) Order(s)	20th Middlesex Regiment Operation Order No 17		
Miscellaneous	20th Middlesex Regt	23/08/1918	23/08/1918
Miscellaneous	Ref. O.O. No 17	23/08/1918	23/08/1918
Operation(al) Order(s)	20th Battalion, Middlesex Regiment. Operation Order No. 18.	26/08/1918	26/08/1918
Operation(al) Order(s)	20th Battalion, Middlesex Regiment. Operation Order No. 19.	31/08/1918	31/08/1918
Heading	War Diary 20th (S) Bn Middlesex Regt. September 1918. Vol 28		
Miscellaneous			
War Diary	Ypres Front	01/09/1918	01/09/1918

War Diary	Frontline.	02/09/1918	05/09/1918
War Diary	Ypres Front Line	06/09/1918	07/09/1918
War Diary	Reserve Orillia Camp.	07/09/1918	11/09/1918
War Diary	Ypres Support Line	12/09/1918	14/09/1918
War Diary	Ypres	14/09/1918	15/09/1918
War Diary	School Camp Sheet 27 L/3.c.5.5.	15/09/1918	20/09/1918
War Diary	Dominion Camp Sheet 28 G23b G24.a.	20/09/1918	26/09/1918
War Diary	Canal Sector	27/09/1918	29/09/1918
War Diary	Smythe Camp	30/09/1918	30/09/1918
Operation(al) Order(s)	Battalion, Middlesex Regiment. Operation Order No. 20.		
Operation(al) Order(s)	Battalion, Middlesex Regiment. Operation Order No. 21.	10/09/1918	10/09/1918
Operation(al) Order(s)	Battn. The. Middlesex Regt. Operation Order No. 22.	14/09/1918	14/09/1918
Miscellaneous	Distribution		
Operation(al) Order(s)	20th Battalion Middlesex Regiment. Operation Order No.25.	20/09/1918	20/09/1918
Operation(al) Order(s)	Middlesex Regiment Operation Order No. 24.	24/09/1918	24/09/1918
Miscellaneous	20th Battalion, Middlesex Regiment. Operation Order No. 25.	26/09/1918	26/09/1918
Miscellaneous	2 1/6 "A" Company.	25/09/1918	25/09/1918
Miscellaneous	Operation Order. By Major W. W. Milne M.C. Commanding Bn. Middlesex Regiment.	27/09/1918	27/09/1918
Miscellaneous	A Form Messages And Signals.		
Miscellaneous	O.C. A Coy 20th middx	28/09/1918	28/09/1918
Miscellaneous	Messages And Signals.		
Miscellaneous	A Form. Messages And Signals.		
Miscellaneous	OC A Coy 20th Middlesex	29/09/1918	29/09/1918
Heading	War Diary 20th Bn Middlesex Regt. October 1918. Vol 29		
War Diary	Smythe Farm.	01/10/1918	01/10/1918
War Diary	Potijze	02/10/1918	11/10/1918
War Diary	Wulverghem	12/10/1918	14/10/1918
War Diary	Werwicq	15/10/1918	17/10/1918
War Diary	Roncq	18/10/1918	18/10/1918
War Diary	Tourcoing	18/10/1918	18/10/1918
War Diary	Mouscron	18/10/1918	20/10/1918
War Diary	Dottignies Espierres	20/10/1918	21/10/1918
War Diary	Front Line	21/10/1918	21/10/1918
War Diary	Dottignies	22/10/1918	23/10/1918
War Diary	Luingne	24/10/1918	31/10/1918
Miscellaneous	Move Orders No.1. O.O No. 28 A	17/10/1918	17/10/1918
Operation(al) Order(s)	Move Orders No 2		
Operation(al) Order(s)	Move Orders No. 3	19/10/1918	19/10/1918
Operation(al) Order(s)	Move Orders No 4	19/10/1918	19/10/1918
Operation(al) Order(s)	Addendum To Move Order No 4	20/10/1918	20/10/1918
Miscellaneous	L'Espierres River		
Miscellaneous	A Form Messages And Signals.		
Operation(al) Order(s)	20th Battn: Middlesex Regt. Operation Order No: 30.	22/10/1918	22/10/1918
Miscellaneous	20th Battalion Middlesex Regiment. Training Programme-Oct. 25th/26th.	25/10/1918	25/10/1918
Miscellaneous	20th Battalion Middlesex Regiment. Training Programme For Week October 28th-November 2nd 1918.	27/10/1918	27/10/1918
Heading	War Diary 20th Middlesex Regt. November 1918 Vol 30		

Type	Description	Start	End
Heading	War Diary. 20th Bn Middlesex Regt November 1918		
War Diary	Luingne	01/11/1918	02/11/1918
War Diary	Petit Audenarde	03/11/1918	08/11/1918
War Diary	Dottignies	08/11/1918	09/11/1918
War Diary	Helchin	09/11/1918	10/11/1918
War Diary	Warcoing	10/11/1918	14/11/1918
War Diary	Warcoing Tourcoing	15/11/1918	17/11/1918
War Diary	Tourcoing	17/11/1918	30/11/1918
Miscellaneous	Move Orders Warning Orders.		
Miscellaneous	Chaplain		
Miscellaneous	Move Orders Warning Orders.		
Miscellaneous	Move Orders	02/11/1918	02/11/1918
Miscellaneous	20th Battalion Middlesex Regiment. Training Programme For Week Ending Nov: 11th, 1918.	11/11/1918	11/11/1918
Operation(al) Order(s)	Bn: Middlesex Regiment Operation Order No: 27.		
Miscellaneous	C.O. 27c T.O. M.O. Qm. Signals All Companies RSM Warning Order.	09/11/1918	09/11/1918
Miscellaneous	A		
Operation(al) Order(s)	Operation Order No: 28	09/11/1918	09/11/1918
Operation(al) Order(s)	Operation Orders No. 29.	10/11/1918	10/11/1918
Operation(al) Order(s)	20th Battalion Middlesex Regiment. Operation Order No. 28.	15/11/1918	15/11/1918
Miscellaneous	20th Battalion, Middlesex Regiment. Orders For Parade For Corps Commander's Inspection.	24/11/1918	24/11/1918
Heading	War Diary. 20th Battn Middlesex Regt. December 1918 Vol 31		
War Diary	Tourcoing	01/12/1918	31/12/1918
Miscellaneous	Army Commander's Inspection. (Practice).	05/12/1918	05/12/1918
Heading	War Diary 20th Battalion Middlesex Regt. January 1919. Vol 32		
Miscellaneous			
War Diary	Tourcoing	01/01/1919	02/01/1919
War Diary	Bondues (Au Jambori)	03/01/1919	05/01/1919
War Diary	Bondues	06/01/1919	31/01/1919
Miscellaneous	All Coys PMC. 2 i/c R.S.M. QM War Diary	02/01/1919	02/01/1919
Miscellaneous	20th Battalion, Middlesex Regiment. Move Orders	02/01/1919	02/01/1919
Miscellaneous	O.C. "A" Company,		
Miscellaneous	Presentation of Colours.		
Miscellaneous	O.C. "A" Company.	29/01/1919	29/01/1919
Miscellaneous	Routine Orders By Lieut: Col: C.E.M. Richards, M.C., Comdg., 20th Middlesex Regt.	29/01/1919	29/01/1919
Heading	War Diary. 20th Battn. Middlesex Regt. February 1919. Vol 33		
Miscellaneous			
War Diary	Bondues	01/02/1919	12/02/1919
War Diary	Fives	12/02/1919	16/02/1919
War Diary	Fives St Andre	16/02/1919	16/02/1919
War Diary	St. Andre	17/02/1919	28/02/1919
Miscellaneous	Notice. 20th Middlesex Regiment Concert Party.		
Miscellaneous	The Scroungers In A Drop Of Black And White. Programme.		
Miscellaneous			
Operation(al) Order(s)	20th Battalion, Middlesex Regiment. Move Order No. 1.	10/02/1919	10/02/1919
Operation(al) Order(s)	20th Battalion, Middlesex Regiment. Move Order No. 2.	11/02/1919	11/02/1919

Type	Description	Date From	Date To
Operation(al) Order(s)	20th Battalion, Middlesex Regiment. Move Order No. 3.	11/02/1919	11/02/1919
Miscellaneous	Standing Orders for Train Guard Arriving From Hazebrouk.	15/02/1919	15/02/1919
Miscellaneous	Administration Staff.	15/02/1919	15/02/1919
Miscellaneous	20th Battalion, Middlesex Regiment. Move Orders.	16/02/1919	16/02/1919
Miscellaneous	Officer Commanding "A" Company.	27/02/1919	27/02/1919
Heading	War Diary 20th Battn Middlesex Regt. March 1919. Vol 34		
Miscellaneous			
War Diary	St. Andr'e Lille.	01/03/1919	31/03/1919
Miscellaneous	20th Battalion, Middlesex Regiment. Move Orders For Army Of Occupation Draft.	01/03/1919	01/03/1919
Heading	35 War Diary 20th Middlesex Regt April 1919. Vol 35		
Miscellaneous			
War Diary	St. Andr'e Lille	01/04/1919	11/04/1919
War Diary	Wattrelos	12/04/1919	30/04/1919
Miscellaneous	20th Battalion, The Middlesex Regiment. Move Orders	10/04/1919	10/04/1919
Heading	War Diary 20th Battn Middlesex Regt May 1919. Vol 36		
Miscellaneous			
War Diary	Wattrelos	01/05/1919	31/05/1919
Heading	War Diary 20th Battn Middlesex Regt 1st-18th June 1919 Vol 37		
Miscellaneous			
War Diary	Wattrelos	01/06/1919	12/06/1919
War Diary	Petit Audenarde	13/06/1919	18/06/1919

WO95/1910

14 Div - 43 Inf Bde

2nd Middx Regt

Jun 1918 - Jun 1919

14TH DIVISION
43RD INFY BDE

20TH BN MIDDX REGT
JUN 1918-JUN 1919

From 40 DIV 121 BDE

Army Form C. 2118.

WAR DIARY
or
INTELLIGENCE SUMMARY.

(Erase heading not required.)

42/14 Vol 23

20th (S) Battalion Middlesex Regt

WAR DIARY

June 1918.

June 1918

WAR DIARY
INTELLIGENCE SUMMARY

20th MIDDLESEX Regt.

JUNE 1918

Place	Date	Hour	Summary of Events and Information	Remarks and references to Appendices
DESVRES	1st Sat.		Arranged training programmes & allotment of instructors with disposition of American Battalions as follows:- 59th US Regiment Regimental Headquarter Company & No I Battalion in DESVRES, No II Battalion in MENNEVILLE, No III Battalion in COURSET. Officers s/r No II Battalion to No I Battalion. Capt R FLOYD to No I Battalion. Training Staff allotted as follows:- Capt. T.W. TRUST at No I Battalion, Capt W.J. MILNE. M.C. & 2/Lt P. WILLIAMS M.C. to No II Battalion. 2/Lt H.J. CLARKE to be in charge of Musketry. 2/Lt MONTAGUE in charge 2/Lt R of LUCAS in charge of Lewis guntraining. 2/Lt CHMONTAGUE in charge of Snipers. NCO's of training staff allottes in proportion. Severe NCO 2/Lt R of LUCAS left behind by the Dublins belong to 16 Instructors in different subjects by this Battalion. different units of the Division taken over by this Battalion. Transport arrives in its afternoon. Decided that Officers of 10 of Battalions should not live with Battalions, but in Messes of Nos II & III Battalion have lunch with them but return for dinner. Whole training staff billeted in DESVRES. Billets very good.	
	2nd Sunday		Church Parade held in the Canteen in DESVRES. No work.	

WAR DIARY
INTELLIGENCE SUMMARY

JUNE 1918

Place	Date	Hour	Summary of Events and Information	Remarks
DE(SY)RES	3rd M.		Working with Americans. Arranging training grounds in the Battalion Areas, together with Rifle Ranges, Lewis gun ranges etc. The Americans found to be very quick & good learners & of very good physique. The officers on the whole were very good, but there was a distinct shortage in the numbers & also of Senior NCOs as these were all away on Courses. Organisation in general is very good.	
	4th 5th 6th 7th F.		Training with Americans.	
	8th		Training with Americans. Orders received that the 59th U.S. Regt would move to-morrow 9th inst. Arrangements made for taking over all stores for training purposes etc. Orders received from 46th Bde that 59th U.S. Regiment moves. 319th U.S. Regiment would arrive at SAMER on Sunday & guides have to be sent for each Battalion & Regt HQrs.	
	9th Sunday		Guides sent to SAMER in the afternoon for Regt HQrs & 1st & II Battalions of 319th U.S. Regiment. These were but little trouble as Saml facilitated by their opposite numbers in the 59th U.S. Regt.	

WAR DIARY or INTELLIGENCE SUMMARY.

Army Form C. 2118.

JUNE 1918.

Place	Date	Hour	Summary of Events and Information	Remarks and references to Appendices
DESVRES	10th		Guides for IIIrd Battalion, 319th US Regiment sent out to meet Battalion, taken to COURSET AREA. Training Staff of the 6th MUNSTER FUSILIERS also arrives & put into this area. They arrived from PALESTINE & handed their battalion over to training staff of MUNSTER Battalion of 16th Division, which was relieved at the same time as we relieved 2nd DUBLINS. Instructors for 6th MUNSTERS to take over from the American Battalion for a few days assist COURSET, our instructors train the Commissioned Officers. Training programme arranges with the Commanding Officer of 319th Regiment — Col COCHEU — who puts himself entirely in our hands until such time as he should receive definite training instructions from his Division. (80th)	
	11th		Training with 319th U.S. Reg't. The whole regiment was literally training – the men though not so big, were nevertheless really better than the 6 9 US – the men were well trained. The officers exceptionally extraordinarily good & well trained. The officers were very enthusiastic & very keen. The whole regiment was very enthusiastic & treated our Staff splendidly, so that training progressed	

WAR DIARY
INTELLIGENCE SUMMARY

Army Form C. 2118.

JUNE 1918

Place	Date	Hour	Summary of Events and Information	Remarks and references to Appendices
DESVRES	11th cont		very rapidly trained. Instructions received that the 8th munsters weren't to carry on with training of American battalion, but that our staff officers were to take over again.	
	12th 13th 14th		Training with Americans, everything very satisfactory indeed. 319th Regt Band played every night in the square opposite our mess.	
	15th		Instructions received that the 16th Division was to proceed overseas to England to form a new division. 20th Division strikes T.S. to-morrow night attached to 7th Division & to move to Boulogne to-morrow night by train for that purpose. Transport to be handed over to 319th US Regiment.	
	16th		Transport handed over to Americans. General farewell taken of American officers. Americans held a duly Battalion Base Ball competition in the afternoon, which was very interesting. Battalion T.S. marches to station at 9.0pm. Marched by 319th Regt Band, which continues to play at the station. Train left DESVRES at 9.65pm with 10	

WAR DIARY
INTELLIGENCE SUMMARY

JUNE 1917

Place	Date	Hour	Summary of Events and Information	Remarks and references to Appendices
DESVRES 16th Camp			Officers 47, O.R. 976 O.R. being full TS establishment, less 3 privates, water cart drivers, mess cart & 4 ASC GS wagon drivers. Arrived at Boulogne approximately at midnight. Officers & an Australian clerk	Arrived at Boulogne
Folkestone Boulogne 17th			marched to dug-outs — remainder live half an hour after the train — the station pickets up lorries which took us to Ostrahove Rest Camp. Left camp at 8.45am. Train entrances at 10.30am. Brn left at 11.15am. Arrived at Folkestone, & had a good crossing, arrived	
ENGLAND			about 1.30pm. Men immediately entrained, due to leave at 4.20pm for Brookwood. Officers lunched at the Pavilion Hotel. Train left at	
BROOKWOOD			4.0pm. Arrived at BROOKWOOD at about 7.0pm. Met by Divisional Staff (14th) & 43rd Brigade Staff, which is our new Brigade. Told that we should become 34th MIDDLESEX over going to BULLSWATER CAMP. Guide led us through P.R. BRIGHT CAMP & this town he had come wrong way. Finally reached BULLSWATER CAMP about 9.0pm.	
BULLSWATER CAMP.	18th Tu.		Camp all canvas, with marquees for Officers messes & Orderly Room to accommodate the whole Brigade. Informed of the general scheme — ie to form nu. battalions of B's & B_2 men; just 4 fortnight trench duties — recalled 34th Middlesex, which at a strength of about 20 officers & 600 men was due to arrive 19th inst.	

WAR DIARY or INTELLIGENCE SUMMARY

Army Form C. 2118.

June 1918.

Place	Date	Hour	Summary of Events and Information	Remarks and references to Appendices
BALLYWATER	18th Cont.		A draft of 740 OR from 3rd F. Surreys & 200 OR from the Buffs arrived at about 4.0 pm. No information previously received as to their arrival. So split up equally among Companies. Bell tents already allotted. 34 hutments except due to arrive in two parties to-morrow night at 11.30 pm & 12.15 am.	
	19th		Preparations for receiving 34th Middlesex. Guides to meet them at BROOKWOOD Station. 1st Party arrives in Camp about midnight. 2nd Party about 1.30 am. Total Strength approximately 22 Officers & 829 OR.	
	20th-7th		Training Staff Klaka overall appointment such as C.O., Adjutant, Training Staff, Company Commanders &c. Staff sent on leave for 7 days. Training Staff had been in France sometime also most those NCO's & men who had recently come from France were convalescents. The Officers of 34th found to have come from every conceivable unit in the British Army. Chief cyclist appointments — 3 all told having been in France before. The men enlisted for Home Service. Organisation of Force men & men entirely unfit for active service. Force men or men entirely unfit for active service. Taken in hand, equipping, informing very difficult owing Klaka of Army experiences of officers. Drafts of 15, 20 & 40 & some continue to arrive from all different battalions. — Bestops, Hants, E. Surrey, Queens, Montgomery Yeomanry etc. One death from Pneumonia.	

WAR DIARY or INTELLIGENCE SUMMARY

JUNE 1918

Place	Date	Hour	Summary of Events and Information	Remarks and references to Appendices
BULLSWATER CAMP	21st–F.		Organisation carried on with & an endeavour made ready to proceed overseas on 30/5 — training impossible owing to & equipping & numerous sick parades of 200 & above. A large number have quite made to carry arms, exempted & wearing equipment battalion quite unable to carry arms. Small drafts continue to arrive & 15 strong and 1000 wounds & & & war establishment, but strength of battalion quickly rises to over war establishment. Camp very badly	
	22nd		equipment only available for War Establishment.	
	23rd		arranged & laid out so that men were able to abstain from work of any sort without being detected. Certain officers apparently NSR very keen to go to France were returned to their depot. NCOTS	
	24/5		sent on leave. An Epidemic of Influenza in the Camp causing large sick parades.	
	25/5		Organisation carried on with as far as possible. NCOs and N/5 arrived a strong Pk up to over 1200 influenza still very bad.	
	26/5		Orders to move on 30/5 received, but cancelled later & more postponed for 3 days. Suspecting DMS to ascertain numbers of unfits Medical Boards held to examine unfits. approximately 50 men passed unfit. Nearly half the remainder unfit owing to influenza	
	27/5		Further Medical Boards held & still more men passed unfit.	
	28/5		In consequence of above 7 MB's it was possible to carry out a little training	
	29/5			

Army Form C. 2118.

WAR DIARY
or
INTELLIGENCE SUMMARY.

(Erase heading not required.)

JUNE 1918

Place	Date	Hour	Summary of Events and Information	Remarks and references to Appendices
BULLSWATER CAMP	30th		All unfits despatched to 225 Mixed Brigade at St Albans. Influenza epidemic still r/o. Training of Remainder carried on. Sick parades very large.	

Melville Roberts Lt Col
Comg 20th If. Bn MIDDLESEX Regt

July 8 / 9 / 18

M 24

WAR DIARY

20th Batty Middlesex Regiment.

July 1918.

WAR DIARY or INTELLIGENCE SUMMARY

20th MIDDLESEX
JULY 1918

Place	Date	Hour	Summary of Events and Information	Remarks and references to Appendices
BULLSWATER CAMP.	1st M.		The Camp having been cleared of the unfits, training proceeded with all day; especially in the matter of Specialists, of which there was a great shortage. Orders received with regard to proceeding overseas – Transport & baggage to go via Southampton, leaving Brookwood on 3rd inst. Personnel to go via Folkestone & Boulogne, leaving Brookwood on 5th inst.	
	2nd		Training continued – Bisley Ranges used all day. Some as yesterday. A further 103 marked as further unfit men were unfit. Medical Board held on more unfits.	A.
	3rd		Training continued – will Range work. Transport entrained in accordance with Operation Orders No. 1. Capt. Westminster went with this party. All officers' valises had to go with the Transport, also QMS Stores, ORm Stores & Messkits &c. Resulting in uncomfortable nights & difficulties in carrying on administration & organisation. A final Medical Board held, and another 16 marks unfit. Preparations for move begun. Training carried on.	
	4.15		Some training in the morning. Final preparations for the move. Battalion to proceed in two trains at 10.35 p.m. & 11.10 p.m. in accordance with Operation Orders No. 2. Last train arrived in FOLKESTONE at about 3.0 a.m. Battalion Strength 39 Officers, 623 OR.	B.

WAR DIARY
INTELLIGENCE SUMMARY.

July 1918

Place	Date	Hour	Summary of Events and Information	Remarks and references to Appendices
FOLKESTONE	5th		Both parties marched to No. 5 Rest Camp & Officers accommodated in surrounding Hotels. - Those in the grand being excessively charged. Paraded at 8 a.m. & marches to the Harbour. The Battalion split up & put half on to one boat & the other half on another. The crossing was very good & landed at Boulogne at about midday. Marched to Ostrohove Rest Camp. Orders for move the following morning received in the evening. Nominal Roll of Officers brought over.	B.1
BOULOGNE	6th		Paraded & marched off at 6 a.m. to Gare Centrale. Entrained here & conveyed to AR Q 15.15, about 7 hours journey. On detraining marched to BOURSIN about 10 miles - Marching not at all bad considering the heat, necessitating a couple of long halts - only 8 men picked up & brought in by the rear party. Officers & men Billeted at BOURSIN. 1st good & scattered. Officers bedrooms scarce, but a certain number of tents made matters better. Transport arrived in the afternoon.	
BOURSIN	7th		Commencement of despatching officers Training commences. & NCO's then on different Courses & schools of Instruction. Weather very good. 40 Division Routine Orders giving Honours & Awards gained by 40 Divisions in the King's Birthday Honours & Gazette 1918	C.

Army Form C. 2118.

WAR DIARY
or
INTELLIGENCE SUMMARY.
(Erase heading not required.)

July 1918

Place	Date	Hour	Summary of Events and Information	Remarks and references to Appendices
BOURSIN.	8th		Training continued, & general organisation. Range at COLEMBERT	
	9th 10th 11th		Training continues - more Courses. Range at COLEMBERT. Training, Commanding Officers and Platoon's Tactical R.B. undergone in the morning. Preparations for move tomorrow.	
JACQUES AREA	11th		Battalion moves to JACQUES AREA - as per Operation order No. 5. Hawker Battalion billets in HARBINGHEM. March completed by noon. Foot & rifle inspections held on arrival. Nobody fell out. Information received from A.D.C Division that 2/Lieut GROVES, who was in the Battalion before its disbandment, had received the Military Cross, is an immediate award for Gallantry in action. This was in the operations of April when this officer 95th was mixed up with 29th Division & was recommended for the above decoration by the Colonel of the 2nd Hants Regt with which Battalion he was fighting.	D
HARBINGHEM	12th	10pm	Battalion moves to NORDAUSQUES as per operation order No. 4. The march took place in short of train pretty well the whole time, 2 men fell out, march completely as per operation order (No. 5). Billets being good indeed.	See April war Diary D1.
NORDAUSQUES	13th	12 noon 2 noon	Battalion moved to ZUDROVE. Spent day in marching as per operation orders (No. 5). Billets fair, but not sufficient. Warning order received for 1 man fell out. Billets in WYNNEZEELE Area on 16th inst. work on the defensive lines; Battalion moved to WYNNEZEELE Area in fortnightly shifts. Remaining two battalions to train, in each Brigade to work on the defences.	D2
ZUDROVE	14th		Cleaning up & fatty at SERQUES. Certain personnel despatches on Courses. Commanding Officers reconnoitred WINNEZEELE LINE with G.O.C. Ammunition to complete 120 rounds per man & Mobile reserve drawn from EPERLECQUES. Preparations for move to-morrow to TATEGHEM AREA; 1st line transports for move by lorry to-morrow to TATEGHEM AREA going March route.	

WAR DIARY or INTELLIGENCE SUMMARY

Army Form C. 2118.

July 1918

Place	Date	Hour	Summary of Events and Information	Remarks and references to Appendices
ZUDAUSVE	15th		Battalion less 1st line Transport, moves by lorry to TERDEGHEM AREA, as per Operation order No.6. left ZUDROVE at 9 am, in 25 lorries taking two day's rations. Officers rations mess kit. arrives at camp positions on CASSEL-STEENVOORDE Road at about 12.30 pm, a found at Army dump Sheet 27. P.3. d. 9.9. for Tents & Trench Shelters waiting. Camp sites chosen at P.4. a. 2.3 for C & D Companies, accommodation Headquarters, A & B Companies. Messes for two Companies & Headquarters & Drums found quite sufficient. Messes for two Companies staged at ZUYPEENE in different farms. Transport staged at ZUYPEENE.	D 3.
TERDEGHEM			The sector of the WINNEZEELE LINE allotted to the Brigade was divided into 3 Sub-sectors, 3 in the morning. All Sub to B (on the right) C (in the Centre) & D Company (on the right), with A Company in Support. All officers reconnoitres the line with Commanding officers. Some steady drill & training carried out. Company officers then Sub-sectors & arrange dispositions for (i) the Company to hold the line until the remainder of the Brigade could arrive, (ii) the battalion which would take over. Tents and Defence scheme for the Shelter Defence of the sector, drawn up. Transport arrived about 11.30 am, having found the pull up to CASSEL rather heavy. Thunderstorm in the night proves the tents as still so good as they looks.	E.
	16th			

Army Form C. 2118.

WAR DIARY
or
INTELLIGENCE SUMMARY.
(Erase heading not required.)

July 1918.

Place	Date	Hour	Summary of Events and Information	Remarks and references to Appendices
TERDEQUIN	17		Working party of approximately 300 all ranks on works during the morning under R.E.'s in the line. Specialist Classes in Lewis gun, Sniping, for Stretcher Bearers carried on. Reconnoitring dispositions in sub-sector continued. Austrian Hundertoferm in the night.	
	18		Working party as yesterday. Training Specialists & reconnoitring also as yesterday. Companies took up positions in the Line in the evening as a practice trench relief.	
	19		Working Parties as usual. Training Specialist Classes & Musketry Platoons firing.	
	20		Working Parties as usual & Specialist Classes. Draft of 232 O.R. arrived at about 5.30 p.m. Sorted out into NCO's, Specialists & soon thus allotted to Companies so as to equalise them as much as possible with Specialists as well as total strengths. A Company had 60. B Company 58. C Company 56. D Company 58. The men on the whole are a bad lot inspite of being catg.g.B.1, but belong to every conceivable regiment in the British Army.	
	21		No work or training. Church Parade at 12 noon.	
	22 23 24 25 26		Working Parties & training carries on Daily. Men payed during the 22nd & 23rd. Division Talks in TERDEGUM made full use of. 35th + 36th Division troupes much enjoyed in the evenings in TERDEQUIN.	

Army Form C. 2118.

WAR DIARY
or
INTELLIGENCE SUMMARY.
(Erase heading not required.)

JULY 1918.

Place	Date	Hour	Summary of Events and Information	Remarks and references to Appendices
FERDEGHEM.	27th		Working Party cancelled owing to rain. Platoon Drill Competition held in the afternoon judged by the Commanding Officer. The best platoon of each Company paraded in Full marching order & drilled in Arms & Close order drill by their own Commander. Points being given for turnout, steadiness in the ranks, drill, arms of command etc. A Company No.1 Platoon under Lt. M. Stephen were the winners but all tried very hard & appeared more or less keen, which was the main thing. A fair amount of football was played during the afternoon — 1st & 2nd section of Medical units was shown during the games.	
	28th		Preparations for relief by M.I. to-morrow begun. In orders will be given to-morrow by hand route taking back by lorries Cancelled later, orders to move by march route to FEDFRXIEFLE 3 days issues issued. Orders for move to-morrow by was to FEDFRXIEFLE issues. Some baggage to Advance party sent right through to No.1 reveille term.	F1 F1
TEROEGHEM - BROXIEFLE	29th		Battalion moved to FEDFRXIEFLE AREA — billets in BROXIEFLE, as per B.O. No.7. & administrative arrangements No.7. In billets by 4:30 p.m. 5 men fell out. It was fortunate being able to sans the great coats forward by lory, as to-day the weather served en route, which gave the troops an excessively Hot. Dinner were served &cided. they fed - at 3:45 p.m. Very Hot.	F2
BROXIEFLE - LE MARAIS.	30th		men about 13/4 hrs rest which they tried very scattered in billets — very scattered. men moved to LE MARAIS; arriving at top of hill overlooking LOTTEN. here rather march. Dinners served on top of hill overlooking pommier. 60 of new fellow most Officers men bathed in Canal on arrival — Cafe — very refreshing,	

Army Form C. 2118.

WAR DIARY
or
INTELLIGENCE SUMMARY.

(Erase heading not required.)

JULY 1918

Place	Date	Hour	Summary of Events and Information	Remarks and references to Appendices
REMARKS -	31st			F 3.
NORTHLEULINGHEM			Battalion moved to NORTHLEULINGHEM, starting at 8.30 am so as to avoid the heat. A very misty morning, forerunner of an extremely hot day. Men marched very well. Arrived at NORTHLEULINGHEM about 11.30 am, only 2 men falling out. Accommodation fair but not as good as expected. Company Commanders discussed. Conference held in the afternoon & general principles of training & preparing for various Competitions in Preparation made for commencing training & preparing for various Competitions in Platoon drill & Firing & Transport etc. 21 Strength of Battalion en route. 39 Officers. 842 O.R.	

July 31st 1918.

O. Mitchell Richards
Comdg 20th MIDDLESEX Regt.

WD July 1918

A Copy No 10

20th Battalion, Middlesex Regiment.

SECRET.

Operation Order No: 1.   2-7-18.

1. The First Line Transport will entrain at BROOKWOOD for conveyance to SOUTHAMPTON, on July 3rd, 1918.

2. The Following personnel, animals, etc., will be carried on this train:—

Officers.	O.R.	Animals.	Vehicles.		Bicycles	Baggage.
			4 wheeled.	2 wheeled.		
2.	50.	55.	14.	4.	9.	5 tons.

3. Captain W.W.MILNE, MC., will be in command of this train, and will report to the R.T.O., on arrival at BROOKWOOD Station.

4. Time of departure 7.35.a.m. Transport will arrive at the station 2 hours before the above time.

5. LOADING PARTIES. The O.C.Duty Company for July 3rd ("B" Coy) will detail the following parties to proceed down to the station with the vehicles, leaving Camp at 5.a.m.
   (a) 1 Officer and 30 men for loading vehicles.
   (b) 1 Officer and 10 men for loading baggage & supplies.
   The O.C. "B" Company will arrange an early breakfast for these men. Officers i/c parties will report to the R.T.O., on arrival at the station.

6. BAGGAGE. Officers' Valises will be stacked outside the Q.M.Stores by 4.30.a.m., July 3rd. Company Mess Kits, Deed Boxes, etc., will be stacked outside the Quartermaster's Stores by 6.p.m., tonight July 2nd. 1 Lorry has been applied for to be at the Q.M.Stores at 4.30.a.m. to convey this baggage to the station. The loading party as detailed in para 5(b) will report to the Quartermaster at 3.p.m. tonight and 4.30.a.m. July 3rd for loading baggage on to 1st Line Transport and the Lorry.

7. The Lewis Gun Officer will be responsible that the Lewis Gun Limbers are loaded this evening, July 2nd.

8. The Medical Officer will be responsible for the loading of the Maltese Cart.

9. Water Carts will be filled before entrainment.
All hay and straw must be removed from the vehicles before entraining, unless completely covered by a sheet. Rifles must not be left on the vehicles, but taken into compartments by the men. Food Bags will be taken into the compartments. Horses and mules, with the exception of pack animals, will be entrained harnessed, unless otherwise ordered.

10. The Officer Commanding the Train will inform the R.T.O., when his unit is completely entrained. He will also make out a warrant for the train load at the R.T.O's office and exchange it for a ticket.

P.T.O..

[signature]
Captain & Adjutant,
20th Battn: Middlesex Regiment.

Distribution:-

Copy No: 1 to O.C. Train.
" No: 2 to Transport Officer.
" No: 3 to Quartermaster.
" No: 4 to O.C. "A" Company.
" No: 5 to O.C. "B" Company.
" No: 6 to O.C. "C" Company.
" No: 7 to O.C. "D" Company.
" No: 8 to Lewis Gun Officer.
" No: 9 to Medical Officer.
" No: 10 to War Diary.
" No: 11. File.

20th Battalion, MIDDLESEX REGIMENT.

Copy No: 11

OPERATION ORDER No: 2.   2nd July, 1918.

1. The Battalion, less 1st Line Transport, and baggage, will entrain at BROOKWOOD on July 4th, for conveyance to FOLKESTONE at the following times:-

    ½ Battalion depart 10.35.p.m. - Train No: X.723.
    ½ Battalion depart 11.10.p.m. - Train No: X.724.

2. The following will be the train loads:-

    Train No: X.723:- "A" & "B" Companies, Headquarter personnel
        Headquarter
            Officers:- The Commanding Officer (O.C.Train)
                Adjutant.
                Quartermaster.
                2/Lieut: C.H.MONTAGUE.

    Train No: X.724:- "C" & "D" Companies. Major J.C.S.Husk,
                                                    (O.C.Train.)
        Headquarter Officers:- Captain C.R.Floyd.
                Lieut: E.C.P.Williams, MC.
                2/Lieut: R.J.Lucas.
                Medical Officer.

3. PARADES. Party for train No: X.723 parade in front of "A" Company's lines, ready to move off, at 8.30.p.m.
Party for train No: X.724 parade in front of "A" Company's Lines, ready to move off, at 9.p.m.
A N.C.O. of each Company who is not proceeding overseas will be present at each companies Roll Call on the above parades, in order to take down particulars of all absentees.

4. RATIONS, for consumption July 5th and 6th will be delivered in Camp on July 4th, and carried on the man.
Water Bottles will be taken filled.

5. Only such baggage as can be carried by hand will be taken, and a certain amount of Orderly Room Stores. I Lorry has been applied for to take this kit to the station.
O.C. Duty Company for July 4th will detail I Officer and 10 men to report at Quartermaster's Stores at 7.30.p.m., July 4th, for loading the Lorry and to load the baggage on the train

6. On the arrival of the units, the Officer Commanding the train load and Officers i/c fatigue parties will report to the R.T.O. When the Unit is ordered on the platform the men will be formed up in fours, facing the carriages. Two fours will be told off to each compartment. Entrainment will commence simultaneously from each end of the train.

7. Detrainment will on no account take place, except by order of the O.i/c Trains.

(Continued)

Operation Order No: 2 dated 2-7-18.
---

8. O.C. Trains will make out a warrant at the R.T.O's office for all personnel on the train. This warrant will be exchanged for a ticket before departure. O.C.Trains will report to the R.T.O. when the unit is completely entrained.

9. DRESS - Full Marching Order. Soft Caps will be worn.

                                              Captain & Adjutant,
                                   20th Battalion Middlesex Regt.

Distribution:-

   Copy No: 1 to O.C. Train No: X.723.
   "   No: 2 to O.C. Train No: X.724.
   "   No: 3 to O.C. "A" Company.
   "   No: 4 to O.C. "B" Company.
   "   No: 5 to O.C. "C" Company.
   "   No: 6 to O.C. "D" Company.
   "   No: 7 to Captain C.R.Floyd.
   "   No: 8 to Quartermaster.
   "   No: 9 to R.S.M.
   "   No: 10 H.Q. Mess.
   "   No: 11 to War Diary.
   "   No: 12 File.

NOMINAL ROLL OF OFFICERS PROCEEDING OVERSEAS.

CO.	Lieutenant Colonel C.E.H. RICHARDS, H.C.	Reg	1st Bn E Lancs Regt
2IC	Major J.C.S. HUSK.	T.F.	6th (Cyc) Bn Hunts
2I/C	Captain C.R. FLOYD.	Temp	20th Middlesex
A	Captain W.W. MILNE, M.C. Temp		
B	Captain F.H. KEATING.	T.F.	1st (R) Bn Camb. & Suffolk Regt
	Captain C. LEAVER.	T.F	City of London Yeo
Adjutant	Captain C. SHEE, M.C. Temp		20th Middlesex
	Hon: Captain & Quartermaster R. STARLING, H.C. Temp		20th Middlesex
C	Lieutenant (A/Captain) T.W. PRUST. Temp		20th Middlesex
Signals	Lieutenant E.C.P. WILLIAMS, H.C. Temp.		
	Lieutenant F. MAXWELL-LAWFORD.	Reg.	1/2 Suffolk Regt
	Lieutenant H.A. STEARN.	T.F.	1st Cambs.
	Lieutenant A.J. GASS.	T.F	4th Suffolk Regt
	Lieutenant H.H. HEADON.	Reg.	R.C.C
T.O	Lieutenant G.V. FRANCIS.	T.F.	2/1st Montgomery Yeo
S.O.S.	2/Lieutenant C.H. MONTAGUE.	Reg.	20th Middlesex
L.G.O	2/Lieutenant R.J. LUCAS.	Temp.	"
	2/Lieutenant H.J. CLARKE.	Temp.	
	2/Lieutenant J.H. EWING.	T.F.	19th R.W. Surreys.
	2/Lieutenant V.E.H. GREEN.	Temp.	5th Middlesex
	2/Lieutenant A.W. BEVAN.	Temp.	51st "
	2/Lieutenant V.W.H. NUNN.	T.F.	19th R.W Surreys
	2/Lieutenant H. RALPH.	Temp.	1/2 R. Sussex
	2/Lieutenant E.V. WILLIAMS.	Temp.	5th Middlesex
	2/Lieutenant E.F. DURHAM.	Temp	32nd "
	2/Lieutenant J. HUNTER.	T.F.	Welsh Horse
	2/Lieutenant A.B. STABLER.	T.F.	City of London Yeo
	2/Lieutenant G.S. BALDWIN.	T.F.	1st (R) Bn. Suffolk Regt
	2/Lieutenant D. APPLEBY.	Temp.	City of London Yeo
	2/Lieutenant P.D. MELVILLE.	T.F.	Welsh Horse
	2/Lieutenant D.A.E. HAMER-JONES.	T.F.	51st Middlesex
	2/Lieutenant F.B. HAWKINS.	Temp	"
	2/Lieutenant H.W. TANNER.	Temp.	1/2 R. Sussex
	2/Lieutenant W. CLARKE.	Temp.	5th Middlesex
	2/Lieutenant F. LoM. CAREY.	Temp	"
	2/Lieutenant E. ATTWATER.	Temp.	"
	2/Lieutenant R.J. MURRAY.	Temp	"
	2/Lieutenant P. BENDA.	Temp	
MO	Captain A.W. EDMONDS, (R.A.M.C.) Temp.		

C

HONOURS & AWARDS
gained by the
20th. (S) Battalion MIDDLESEX Regt.
in the
King's Birthday Honours Gazette 1918.

Lt.Col C.E.M. RICHARDS M.C. — Mention.
Capt.Adjt. L. PRICE (since W&P of W April 1918) — Mention.
Capt. C. SMEE — M.C.
51166 Sgt. (C.S.M) J. MILLER — M.S.M.
14420 Cpl. F. CRANE (since missing April 1918) — D.C.M.
6821 Cpl. E. MARTIN (since missing April 1918) — M.S.M.

Lt. J. COWPER (wounded November 1917) — Mention.
Capt. T.Q.M. R. STARLING (from 11th Lanc Fus) — M.C.

To:- O.C. "A" Company,
       "B" Company,
       "C" Company,
       "D" Company,
       Transport Officer

~~WAR DIARY~~

Reference Operation Order No: 3 dated 10-7-18, para 4, last sentence, read:-

"The Mess Cart will be at Headquarters at 6.a.m. "C" Company will send their Mess Kit to Headquarters by that time".

Soft Caps will be worn on the March.

Captain & Adjutant,
20th Battalion, Middlesex Regiment.

10-7-18.

20th Battalion, Middlesex Regiment.

Copy No: 13

OPERATION ORDER No. 3.   10-7-18.

MAP: CALAIS 13.

    Reveille:- 5.a.m.
    Sick:-   5.15.a.m.
    Breakfast:-5.30.a.m.

1. The Battalion will move to LICQUES Area (HOCQUINGHEN and HARBINGHEN) tomorrow, by march route.
   Order of March:- H.Q., "C", "D", Drums, "A", "B", Transport.

2. The Head of the Column will pass "A" Company's Billet at 6.45.a.m.

3. Intervals, as follows, will be maintained:-
   200 yards between Companies, and "B" Company & Transport.

4. Officers' Valises will be at Quartermaster's Stores by 6.p.m. Transport Officer will send a Limber to collect H.Q. Officers' Valises at 5.45.a.m. The Mess Cart will collect Mess Kit, commencing with "D" Company at 6.a.m.

5. ADVANCE PARTIES. 1 N.C.O. per Company and 1 for H.Q., who can ride a bicycle will report to 2/Lieut: C.H. MONTAGUE at "A" Company's Billet at 6.a.m., with Bicycles, to proceed in advance.

6. SICK. Field Ambulance will collect 1 hour before Units march off. Any men considered by the Medical Officer unfit to march, will report to the Transport Officer at 6.30.a.m., as brakesmen. Such men will have a chit signed by the Medical Officer.

7. RATIONS. 14th M.T. Company will dump Supplies at LICQUES Church at 2.p.m., 11th instant, to be drawn for consumption 13th instant, by Supply Wagons at 6.p.m., tomorrow.

8. DINNERS, will be served on arrival in new area.

9. Officers Commanding Companies will personally inspect all Billets occupied by their men and see that they are scrupulously clean. They will report to the Adjutant that they have done this before moving off. All tents will be left standing.

10. Officers Commanding Companies will report to the Adjutant, immediately on arrival, the number of Other Ranks who fell out on the Line of March.

                                (sd) COLIN SHEE, Captain & Adjutant,
                                   20th Battalion, Middlesex Regiment.

Distribution:-

```
Copy No: 1    Commanding Officer.
 "    "  2    Adjutant.
 "    "  3    Second in Command.
 "    "  4    O.C. "A" Company.
 "    "  5.   O.C. "B" Company.
 "    "  6    O.C. "C" Company.
 "    "  7    O.C. "D" Company.
 "    "  8.   Quartermaster.
 "    "  9    Transport Officer.
 "    " 10    Medical Officer.
 "    " 11    2/Lieut: C.H. MONTAGUE.
 "    " 12    R. S. M.
 "    " 13    War Diary.
 "    " 14    File.
```

20th Battalion, Middlesex Regiment.

SECRET

OPERATION ORDER No: 4.   11th July, 1918.

Ref: CALAIS 13.
     HAZEBROUCK.5.

1. The Battalion will move to NORDAUSQUES, tomorrow, July 12th, by march route.   Order of March:-
       H.Q., "B", "C", Drums, "D", "A", Transport.

2. The Head of the column will pass the Orderly Room at 7.a.m. Usual intervals will be maintained. Dress, as for to-day. O.C. "A" Company will detail a rear party of 1 Officer and 12 Other Ranks.

ROUTE.   CANCHY - CLERQUES - BONNIQUES LEZ ARDRES, approximately 7½ miles.

4. Officers' Valises will be at the Quartermaster's Stores, ready for loading at 6.a.m. Mess Kit will be collected as follows:- "A" Company and H.Q., at 6.a.m. "C", "B" and "D" Companies at Company Messes: all Mess Kitt to be ready by 6.15.a.m.

5. ADVANCE PARTIES.   The usual Advance Partys with bicycles will report to 2/Lieut: C.H.MONTAGUE at Orderly Room at 6.a.m. to rpoceed in advance, and report to the Area Commandant at TOURNEHEM.

6. Rations for consumption 14th instant will be dumped at TOURNEHEM CHURCH at 4.p.m., 12th instant. G.S. Wagons will refill at 7.p.m.

7. Dinners will be served in New Area.

8. O.C. Companies will personally inspect all billets occupied by their men and see that they are scrupulously clean. They will report this to the Adjutant before moving off. On arrival Officers Commanding Companies will report immediately the number of O.Ranks who fell out on the Line of March.

10. Orders about Tents will be issued later.

                    (sd.) COLIN SHEE, Captain & Adjt:
                          20th Battalion, Middlesex Regiment.

Distribution:-

Copy No: 1 - O.C. "A" Company,
No: 2 - O.C. "B" Company,
No: 3 - O.C. "C" Company,
No: 4 - O.C. "D" Company,
No: 5 - Second in Command.
No: 6 - Adjutant,
No: 7 - Quartermaster,
No: 8 - Transport Officer.
No: 9 - Medical Officer.
No: 10 - R.S.M.
No: 11 - 2/Lieut: C.H.MONTAGUE.
No: 12 - War Diary.
No: 13.- File.

20th Battalion, Middlesex Regiment.

Copy No: 12

SECRET   OPERATION ORDER NO: 5.   12-7-18.

D2.

Ref: HAZEBROUCK, 5.a.

1. The Battalion will move, by march route, to ZUDROVE tomorrow, 13th instant.
    Order of March:- H.Q., "A", "B", Drums, "C", "D", Transport.

2. The Head of the column will pass the cross roads immediately North of the 2nd U in NORDAUSQUES at 8.50.a.m. Usual intervals to be maintained.
    10 minutes halt to be made every 20 minutes.
    Dress:- As for to-day.   O.C. "D" Company will detail a rear party of 1 Officer and 12 Other Ranks.

3. Officers' Valises will be at the Quartermaster's Stores at 7.45.a.m. Mess Kit will be stacked at the Quartermaster's Stores, ready for loading by 8.a.m.

4. ADVANCE PARTIES. The usual Advance Parties with bicycles will report to 2/Lieut: C.H.MONTAGUE at Headquarters at 7.a.m., and proceed in advance, and report to Area Commandant, at WATTEN.

5. Sick will be collected by 43rd Field Ambulance 1 hour before the Battalion moves off.

6. SUPPLIES. Refilling Point on 13th instant and onwards will be at 2.p.m., at EPERLECQUES.

7. Baggage and Supply Wagons will remain with the Unit after the move.

8. D.A.D.O.S. Dump and Office will be at WATTEN. Ordnance Supplies will be delivered to Supply Refilling Point by D.A.D.O.S., and will drawn from there by 1st Line Transport.

9. Paras: 7 and 8 of Operation Order No: 4 will be adhered to.

10. On arrival in the New Area, Foot and Rifle Inspections will be held under Company arrangements, and by 2/Lieut: R.J.LUCAS for Headquarters.

(sd) Colin Smee Capt/Adjt.
20th Batn. Middlesex Regt.

Distribution:-

    As per Operation Order No: 4.

20th Battalion, Middlesex Regiment.

D3
Copy No 12.

SECRET.

Operation Order No: 6.   14-7-18.

Ref: Sheets (27.a.S.E.- 1/20,000.
             (27.   - 1/40,000.
             (HAZEBROUCK, S.a.

1. The Battalion less Transport, will move by Lorry at 9.a.m. tomorrow, June 15th, to TERDEGHEM for work on the WINNEZEELE LINE, under C.R.E., 14th Division.

2. Lorries are allotted as follows:-
   5 per Company and 5 for Headquarters, for personnel, Officers' and Baggage. Officers' valises, Mess Kit, rations for 15th and 16th instant and 5 boilers per Company and H.Q., will be taken on the baggage lorries. 4 Lorries will be allotted to the men and 1 for Officers and baggage.

3. EMBUSSING. Captain C.R.FLOYD will be the Embussing Officer. The Lorry convoy will form up on the road from SERQUES through R.7.c. and R.13.a., the head of the column facing north at R.7.c.4.8.
   Embussing will take place in the following order:-
   Headquarters, "A", "B", "C", "D". Companies will march on to the convoy in this order at 8.30.a.m..
   The Transport Officer will detail a limber per Company and one for Headquarters to collect Officers' valises and Mess boxes by 8.a.m. and convey them to the above road by 8.30.a.m. Kit that cannot be got on this limber will be man handled to the road at the same time.

4. Transport will move by route march, under orders of the Transport Officer to TERDEGHEM, staying night of 15/16th instant at NORDPEENE; billets to be obtained from Area Commandant. They should leave present billets by 10.a.m.

5. Baggage not taken on the lorries will be loaded on to the 1st Line Transport by 8.a.m. tomorrow, July 15th. Band Instruments will be carried by 1st Line Transport.

6. Men earmarked for inspection by Inspector of Drafts will not rpoceed with the Battalion. They will be left behind under the charge of 2/Lieutenant R.S.MURRAY, to whom nominal rolls will be handed in triplicate. These men will be collected together in one billet under the orders of 2/Lieut: R.S.MURRAY, after the Battalion has left. 2/Lieut: R.S.MURRAY will parade all these men at the Transport Lines at 8.30.a.m. to load 1st Line Transport vehicles. Rations for this party will be delivered at No: 43 Billet for 17th and onwards, by 41st Brigade. Rations for 15th and 16th instants will be issued by the Quartermaster.

7. Rations for consumption 17th instant will be delivered in the new area.

(sd) COLIN SMEE, Captain & Adjt:
20th Battalion, Middlesex Regt.

E.

20th Battalion, The Middlesex Regiment.   SECRET.

SKELETON DEFENCE SCHEME.   43rd Brigade Sector.

Ref: Sheet 27 N.E.   Western Edit.
     27.S.E.

1. 20th Middlesex Regiment, to be known as "A" Battalion, will hold 43rd Brigade Sector, as Skeleton Defence.
   In case of enemy attack, they will be prepared:-
   (a) To hold the line.
   (b) Have guides in readiness to guide troops to any position in Brigade Sector. The H.L.I., and 12th Suffolks Regiment will be known as "B" and "C" Battalions respectively.
   (c) When "B" & "C" are in occupation of Line, move into reserve at J.31.d.

2. The Boundaries of the Sector are:-
   (a) North, Line drawn from J.24.b.00.40 to J.23.b.90.40.
   (b) South, Line drawn from P.6.c.80.25. to N.4.c.60.30.
   The 78th American Division are on the left and 42nd Brigade (6th Wiltshire Regt) 14th Division on the Right.

3. The Brigade Sector is divided into three sub-sectors, which would normally be a Battalion front.
   As a Skeleton Defence, each Battalion front will be held by one Company, ½ Company will be kept in reserve, astride CASSEL - STEENWOORDE Road at P.5.b.a.d.; and ½ Company at FOCH FARM.

4. Boundaries of Battalion fronts are:-
   RIGHT COMPANY:-
       Right - P.6.c.80.25 to P.3.c.50.25.
       Left - J.35.a.70.15. along track exclusive to
              J.34.d.85.50. then S.W. to J.33.d.30.20.
   CENTRE COMPANY - Right - J.35.a.70.15. along track inclusive to
              J.34.d.85.50. then S.W. to J.33.d.30.20.
           Left - J.28.b.45.20. track inclusive to
              J.27.d.65.70. then to J.27.c.65.20.
   LEFT COMPANY - Right - J.28.b.45.20. track exclusive to
              J.27.d.65.70. then to J.27.c.65.20.
           Left - Line drawn from J.22.b.00.40. to
              J.26.b.80.00.

5. The Defence of each Sub-Sector will be organised in depth. It is suggested that where ground is suitable, one platoon will hold Picquet Line, two platoons Front Line, One platoon Support Line. Lewis Guns will normally remain with their Platoons, and they will be sited so as to obtain best results from flanking and enfilade fire. It will generally be found advantageous for these Guns to be located in positions in rear or front of actual lines of trenches.

6. The chief points of tactical importance are:-
   (1) High Ground round MILL at P.4.b.55.00.
   (2) RWELD VILLAGE and Ridge.
   These positions should be organised for all round defence, and should be held at all costs.

7. The principles of defence are:-
   Picquet Line is to be held lightly, but it must be understood that troops holding this line will hold out to the last, to delay and disorganise the enemy's attack as much as possible. This Line will not normally be reinforced, but every effort should be made to eject any isolated small party of enemy which should enter it. If this Line is captured and held in strength by the enemy, every effort will then be made to concentrate on defence of Front or Main Line. The main system of defence is the Front Line in rear of Picquet Line. This Line will be held at all costs and should the enemy penetrate it he will be

immediately ejected by quick counter-attacks by support Platoons or Companies. Great importance is attached to these Counter-attacks being rapidly carried out.

8. Along practically the whole of the front the field of fire is very poor owing to growth of corn. O.C. Sub-sectors will so arrange their posts that positions are chosen so as to obtain the best fire results. It may be necessary to cut diagonal lanes in the corn, which would be guarded by Lewis Gun. Ground will be carefully reconnoitred with a view to cutting these lanes.

9. All ditches, Dykes and low ground will be watched, as the enemy is carefully trained in taking advantage of ground in his advances.

10. This Cancels previous Defence Schemes issued

                          Captain & Adjutant,
               20th Battalion, Middlesex Regiment.

22-7-18.

20th Battalion Middlesex Regiment.

SECRET.

AMENDMENT to SKELETON DEFENCE SCHEME issued 22-7-18.

Para 3, 1st Line - for "three" read "two"

2nd Line - after "as a skeleton defence" erase "each - - - - - one Company" and substitute " the front will be divided into 5 Sub-sectors, each Sub-sector being held by one Company"

[signature]
Captain & Adjutant,
20th Battalion Middlesex Regiment.

23-7-18.

Copy No: 10

20th Battalion, Middlesex Regiment.
―――――oOOo―――――

SECRET.

Operation Order No: 7,   28-7-18.

Ref: Sheet 27 1/40,000.
HAZEBROUCK 5.a. 1/100,000.
Sheets 27.a. S.E. & N.E. 1/20,000.

1. The Battalion will move to NORTBEULINGHEM by march route, via LEDERZEELE and LES MARAIS, on July 29th, 30th and 31st, in accordance with attached Time-table.

2. Approximate time of moving will be 9.a.m. daily.

3. The following intervals will be maintained throughout the march.
   Between Companies - 100 yards.
   Between Rear Company and Transport - 100 yards.
   Between each section of 6 vehicles - 25 yards.

4. The O.C. of the Rear Company each day will detail a Rear Party of one Officer and 12 Other Ranks to march in rear of the column.

5. ADVANCE PARTIES. 2/Lieutenant C.H.MONTAGUE and the Interpreter and 1 N.C.O. per Company and Headquarters (able to ride a bicycle) will proceed in advance daily to arrange accommodation, reporting as under for billets in the new areas:-
   July 29th - Leave present Camp 8.30.a.m. and report to Area Commandant, LEDERZEELE (Sub Area B) for accommodation, night 29th/30th.
   July 30th - Report to Area Commandant, WATTEN, for accommodation in LES MARAIS night 30/31st before leaving on LEDERZEELE at 8.30 a.m.
   July 31st - Leave LES MARAIS 8.30.a.m. and report to Area Commandant, EPERLECQUES for accommodation in NORTBEULINGHEM.

6. March Times will be 10 minutes halt every 50 minutes.
   Strict March Discipline will be maintained..

7. O.C. Companies will report arrival in billets immediately to Orderly Room, on completion of each day's march.
   Foot inspection will be held by Platoon Commanders on completion of each day's march.

8. Further Administrative arrangements will be issued for each day's move.

(sd) COLIN TMEE, Captain & Adjutant,
20th Battalion, Middlesex Regiment.

DISTRIBUTION:-
Copy No: 1 - O.C. "A" Company.
"   2 - O.C. "B" Company.
"   3 - O.C. "C" Company.
"   4. - O.C. "D" Company.
"   5 - Adjutant.
"   6 - Quartermaster.
"   7 - Transport Officer.
"   8 - 2/Lieutenant C.H.MONTAGUE.
"   9 - R. S. M.
"   10 - War Diary.
"   11 - File.

MARCH TABLE.
-oOo-

Date.	Order of March.	Time of moving off.	Route.	Remarks.
July 29th.	H.Q., "B", "C" Drums, "D", "A", Transport.	Head of column to pass corner P.S.b.2.3. at 9.a.m.	CASSEL, WEMAES-CAPPEL, BAMBECQ, LEDRINGHEM.	Dinners to be served at H.35 d, at 12.30 pm 2 hours rest allowed.
July 30th	H.Q., "C", "D" Drums, "A", "B" Transport.	to be notified later.	in HARIS.	Dinners probably served in L.H.H.
July 31st	H.Q., "D", "A" Drums, "B", "C", Transport.	to be notified later.	HOULLE, WATTALIMHES.	Dinners probably served in new Area.

ADMINISTRATIVE ARRANGEMENTS. Copy No: 11
to
OPERATION ORDER, No: 7.
28-7-18.

Orderly Officer:- 2/Lieutenant W.Clark.
Company for duties:- "C"

Reveille:- 5.45.a.m.
Sick Parade:- 6.a.m.
Breakfast:- 6.15.a.m.

1. Two Lorries for conveyance of Baggage and Advance Party direct to NORTLEULINGHEM will report at 7.a.m. July 29th and rejoin their Units on completion of duty.

2. ADVANCE PARTY. Major W.W.MILNE, MC, and one N.C.O. per Company and Headquarters will proceed as Advance Party to take over Billets and and Stores, Practice S.A.A., etc., from H.L.I., These N.C.O's with Full Equipment and three days rations will report to Quartermaster at 6.30.a.m. to assist in loading. This does not cancel the advance party proceeding to LEDERZEELE. The Advance Party proceeding from LE MARAIS to NORTLEULINGHEM on July 31st (O.O. No: 7 para 5) is cancelled.

3. BAGGAGE. The following to be carried by these Lorries will be stacked at the Quartermaster's Stores at 6.45.a.m.:-
Blankets, in bundles of 10 and labelled: Company Deed Boxes and Mob" Stores: Washing Tins, Targets, Band Rifles and Packs, Orderly Room Stores.

4. OFFICERS' VALISES, will be stacked at Quartermaster's Stores ready for loading at 8.a.m. The Mess Cart will collect Mess Kit only, commencing with "C" Company at 8.15.a.m.

5. LOADING PARTIES. O.C. "A" Company will detail a party of 2.N.C.O's and 12 men to load Baggage as in para 3 above, to report to Quartermaster at 6.45.a.m. O.C."B" Company will detail a party of 2 N.C.O's and 12 men to load Baggage as in para 4 above to report to Quartermaster at 8.a.m.

6. WATER CARTS, will be taken half full. Water Bottles will be carried full.

7. AS LITTLE Baggage as possible should be unloaded after each day's march to avoid unnecessary labour next morning.

8. RATIONS. The 50th Division will deliver supplies in this Area for day after departure. The 14th Divisional Train will deliver supplies for consumption July 31st at LE MARAIS on July 30th and for consumption August 1st at NORTLEULINGHEM on July 31st.
1st Line Transport will draw rations on and after August 1st from Refilling Point at HELLEBROUCQ at 2.p.m. daily.

9. DINNERS. Headquarters and Transport Dinners for each day will be arranged as follows:-
Headquarters:- Band, Signallers, and Pioneers with "A" Company. Remainder with "B" Company.
Transport:- A.S.C. Drivers and Leaders, Grooms, Shoemakers and Tailors with "C" Company. Remainder with "B" Company.
The Transport Officer and R.S.M. will arrange for rations to be handed over accordingly.

10. OVERCOATS will be rolled in bundles of 10, labelled, and stacked at Quartermaster's Stores by 7.15.a.m. for conveyance direct to LEDERZEELE by Lorry, reporting at 7.30.a.m. Quartermaster will supply personnel to conduct same.

(sd) COLIN SMEE, Captain & Adjutant,
20th Battalion Middlesex Regiment.

Appendix

Administrative Orders No 2
to Operation Order No 7.

Ref Sheet 27 1/40,000.

    Orderly Officer 2/Lt H Raeph
    Reveille :— 6 am.
    Sick :— 6-15 am.
    Breakfast — 6-30 am.

1. The Battalion will move to Le Marais tomorrow July 30th.

2. Order of March. Headquarters, "C" "D" Drums "A" "B" Transport. Head of column will pass road-junction at G 22. b. 90. 70. at 9 am.

3. Officers' valises will be collected and loaded by Officers' servants as follows:— Headquarters & A, B & D Coys at Orderly Room at 8 am — "C" Coy at "C" Coy's H.Q. at 8.30 am. Officers' servants will not leave the valises until they are properly loaded

Mess Kit will be collected by Mess Cart commencing with "A" Coy at 8 am.

4. Water Carts and water bottles will be taken filled.

5. Attention is drawn to paras. 3, 4, 6 and 7 of O.O. No 7.

6. <u>Advance party.</u> As laid down in para. 5 of O.O. No 7. NCO's will report to 2/Lieut Montague at Orderly Room at 8-30 am with bicycles.

7. Dinner & tea rations of H.Q. and Transport will be handed over as laid down in para. 9. of Administrative arrangements issued on 28th instant. Dinners for tomorrow will be served en route.

8. <u>Loading party.</u> OC "C" Coy will detail a loading party of 1 Officer and 20 other ranks, to load great-coats to report to Q.M. at 7.45 am.

9. <u>Parade States</u>. OC Coys will be prepared to furnish a parade state by 9 am tomorrow. This will be produced when called for.

10. OC Coys will ensure that the order prohibiting men walking about outside their billets without puttees is brought to the notice of all ranks on arrival in new area. This breach of discipline was particularly noticeable today.

29/7/18

(Sgd.) Colin S mee.
Captain & Adjutant.
20th Battn Middlesex Regt

Administrative Orders No 3.
to Operation Orders No 7

ADJUTANT
F3

Ref: Hazebrouck 5A 1/100,000

Orderly Officer 2/Lt. J.W. Ewing
Company for Duty "A"

Reveille   5-30 a.m.
Sick   5-45 a.m.
Breakfast   6-0 a.m.

1. The Battalion will move to NORTLEULINGHEM in accordance with O.O. No 7.

2. The Head of Column will pass the road junction 550x S.W. of pt 45 just S in SERQUES at 8-30 a.m.

3. Officers Valises will be collected as follows:—
H.Q. B & C at Headquarters at 7 a.m.
A Coy at 7-15 a.m.
D Coy at 7.45 a.m.
Valises will be loaded by Officers Servants.
The Mess Cart will collect Mess Kit of H.Q. B & C Coys at Headquarters at 7-15 a.m. A Coy at 7-30 a.m. & D Coy at 8-0 a.m.

values when kit must be ready by
the above times.

4. Dinner will be served at
NORTLEULINGHEM.

5. Attention is drawn to paras 3. 4.
6 & 7 of O.O. No 7 & to paras
4 - 9 & 10 of administrative Order
No 2. issued yesterday.

(Sgd) Colin Tower
Captain H/Captains
30-7-18   20th Middlesex Regt

Distribution:-

    Copy No: 1 - O.C. "A" Company.
    "   2 - O.C. "B" Company.
    "   3 - O.C. "C" Company.
    "   4 - O.C. "D" Company.
    "   5 - Adjutant.
    "   6 - Quartermaster.
    "   7 - Transport Officer.
    "   8 - Major W.W.MILNE, MC.
    "   9 - 2/Lieutenant G.H.MONTAGUE.
    "   10 - R. S. M.
    "   11 - War Diary.
    "   12.- File.

WAR DIARY

20th Battalion Middlesex Regiment.

August 1918.

Army Form C. 2118.

WAR DIARY
or
INTELLIGENCE SUMMARY.
(Erase heading not required.)

Place	Date	Hour	Summary of Events and Information	Remarks and references to Appendices

Instructions regarding War Diaries and Intelligence Summaries are contained in F. S. Regs., Part II. and the Staff Manual respectively. Title pages will be prepared in manuscript.

Army Form C. 2118.

WAR DIARY
or
INTELLIGENCE SUMMARY.
(Erase heading not required.)

— AUGUST 1918 —

Place	Date	Hour	Summary of Events and Information	Remarks and references to Appendices
NORTLEULINGHEM	1st	8.30am	Platoon & Company Training & Specialist classes carried on. Various personnel sent on courses. Games in the afternoon. 2/Lt. J. MURRAY & men of PATZWOOGVE reported, less 19 sent down to base. Classified blows B, by M.I.D.	
	2nd	12.30pm	Same as yesterday. Transport preparing for horseshow on Aug 5th. Some gas put up & medical inspection for contagious diseases. None very good.	
	3rd	8.30am – 12.30pm	Some of the Officers riders tried over the jumps for horseshow. Medical inspection for contagious diseases held in all Companies. Brigade Drill Competition for best platoon in the Bde was won by No 1 Platoon, under Lt H.A. STORM, which was judged by G.O.C, Brigade & 3 other O.C.s scoring total of 81 points against Lt F.I. 76 pts 15 & 12th Suff Btks. 72 pts. 15.	A.
	4th	9.30am 10.30am	Church Parade. Vehicles competing in Brigade Transport Competition judged by O. No 24 Company Dist / Train. Very good turn out considering the 3 days trek before hand. The limbers won first prize, & considered that the horses were not well groomed. Cookers & Cooker were all 2nd.	
	5th	4.0pm	The pack pony tied with 12th Suffolks. The Mess Cart, Charger & Cooker was inspected by Lt Col JAMES. All officers & NCOs per Coy HQ attended a lecture at MOBILE on Aeroplanes by Lt Col JAMES. No Parades. Divisional Horseshow at EPERLECQUES. Entries made for following events "Cooker" Limber, "Water Cart", "Mess Cart", "Pack Pony", "Pair (H.T.) Horses, Officers Charger Open", a Jumping - Open & Officers Charger Open. The Cookers being placed Second. Ridden by Coy Commander of Suffolks. One prize only was won. The Cookers being placed Second & 14th Division Entry. Total points scored in first 6 events enumerated above being 353.	B.
	6th	2-30	Company Training. Second Army demonstration Platoon gave a demonstration to as many Officers & NCOs as possible at INGHINGHEM MILL (Sheet 27.A.S.E. P24 C.10.9.5) Hard drive of arms, Platoon training, advance in an attack on a Strong point, latter very good, but turn out not particularly impressive. Gas demonstration by O.G. of platoon & lecture. All Officers in evening.	

WAR DIARY
INTELLIGENCE SUMMARY

Army Form C. 2118.

August 1918.

Place	Date	Hour	Summary of Events and Information	Remarks and references to Appendices
HERTFEUILLEMONT.	7th		Company training carried on. Practice of D Company in an attack on Inghem Mill. Platoon & Company Commanders & other Officers to a demonstration on training by Sgt Snow Masse at HERDEGHEM - very good demonstration.	
	8th		Company Training. D Company gain practice attack, which is to done before Army Commander present to-day. No 7 Platoon for division to-morrow. Army Commander present to-day. No 7 Platoon practising on Range for shooting Competition.	
	9th		D Company Carried out attack. Two strong points were taken. First one under cover of T.M (Stokes) barrage, smoke & rifle grenades (all live rounds) & using many L.g.m & Lewis rifle ammunition. This was quite well done & q shooting was very good. attack on second point not so good - attackers seeming to forget what they were supposed to do. Very useful piece of training nevertheless. Brigade staff to dinner.	
	10th		Platoon Shooting Competition at 10.30 am. 2 Companies on range in S.D. kit remainder usual training. No 7 Platoon won the competition scoring 93 points, 12th Suffolks scoring 89 points. No 1 Platoon preparing for special Church Parade at HERDEGHEM to-morrow, where His Majesty The King will be present to represent 11th & 43rd Bde.	

WAR DIARY or INTELLIGENCE SUMMARY

Army Form C. 2118.

August 1915

Place	Date	Hour	Summary of Events and Information	Remarks and references to Appendices
NORTHUNGHAM	11th		No 1 Platoon to TATTERSHALL by Lorry early in the morning. Command Pay Officer leave warrants. Commanding Officer attended Divisional Parade in the morning. Regimental Sports in the afternoon. 12th Suffolks were invited & good many turns up. Tea provided on the ground. Prizes presented on the ground. Battalion concert given in the evening - very good afternoon & evening for men to move to men's entertainment. Preparations also made for move tomorrow of Battalion equipment.	C
	12th		Moved to MARAIS - leaving NORTHUNGHAM at 7.30 am. 4 lorries provided to assist in carrying baggage, as men made it very hot. Kept it but all in billets by 10.45 am. Same billets as previously. Baths & clean clothes available for all from 10.0 am. Whole Battalion bathed & had clean change of linen on march. 2 men fell out on march. Most men also bathed in Canal.	C1
LES MARAIS	13th		Moved to BROXEELE, leaving billets 7.0 am - all in billets by 10.30 am. One man fell out just outside EVERSAELE having sprained his ankle. Weather escaped the very hot midday.	
BROXEELE	14th		Moved to ESQUELBECQ AREA. Billets & accommodation not at all good being insufficient & very scattered. The longest & hottest march yet done.	C2

WAR DIARY or INTELLIGENCE SUMMARY

Army Form C. 2118.

August 1918

Place	Date	Hour	Summary of Events and Information	Remarks and references to Appendices
SQUEREGQ.	15th		Moved to DROGLANDT AREA. A very hot march after previous 3 days marching, beginning to tell on the men - with weak legs. Arrived in new area about 11.30 a.m. 3 O.R. having fallen out. Found billets again were very scattered, insufficient upon. Tents obtained gallantly proportionately. Headquarters being entirely under canvas. Patrol work carried out in the evening.	C.3
DROGLANDT	16th		Training carried on in the morning, by Companies. II Corps (Commander inspected 1 Company (C Company), all Company Commanders & the Staff at 3.0 p.m.	C.4.
"	17th		Moved to PROVEN AREA, starting 7.0 a.m. arriving at 10 a.m. Battalion split up into 3 different Camps; H.Q. 9A at PIGEON (south) F.14.a.4.3, B & D under Canvas at 27/F.8.c.1.3 PRESTWICH, C in huts at 27/F.7.d.7.5. MELEAN. Transport this near C Company. Plenty of room. Commanding Officer proceeded up to reconnoitre the line, by car from Bde. H.Q at B ROGLANDT, returning to PIGEON Camp at about 2.0 p.m. Orders for move to motors received from Brigade. Personnel to Lory rail to SIEGE Camp, shut 28/8.27.a.4.6. Transport by Road to 28/9.4.c.4.9. Van got that 5 + 9 Limbers, Cookers, Water Carts of Battle to go to Siege Camp. Lorry to Convey Officers valises & kit to Siege Camp on to assist move blankets etc to new T/Post	C.5.
SIEGE CAMP	18th		Guess Kit to Siege Camp early. Battalion arrived at Camp about 10 a.m. & relieves 1/5 K.O.Y.L.I.S, in lines. Reserve area of 49th Division. O.C. Companies, 2nd in command, & M.O. Lipig	

Army Form C. 2118.

WAR DIARY
or
INTELLIGENCE SUMMARY.
(Erase heading not required.)

August 1918

Place	Date	Hour	Summary of Events and Information	Remarks and references to Appendices
Siege Camp Cont	19		proceeded by lorry from Brigade HQ in Proven, Billets etc being taken over from 4th York & Lancs on night 19th/20th in Right Sector of 49th Division Front. Arrived Packenham Camp about 2.30pm. Transport Officer & Quartermaster having gone by road & been given T/off was withdrawn, motorised vehicles at about 1.10pm. Arrangements made for removing surplus baggage to "hot" lines to lorries etc to Ravens, obtained 15 or 16 deliveries in Rear Camps by M.T., and put at T/off lines had to be brought forward by Bgd. wagons, thus much delayed. Administrative instructions with regard to baggage etc issued at Bde HQ at 5.15 pm.	D
			Commanding Officer for conference at their HQ in the morning. Commanding Officer spoke to the men on the general situation & their near future. Subaltern Officers on their trench duties. Preparing tomorrow up the line. Gas & Patrol training carried out in the morning.	D1
Right Brigade Sector Ypres.	19/20	8.0pm	Left Camp & proceeded to Railhead Trois Tours & proceeded up the line in trains. Relief proceeded smoothly & complete by 12.30 am Aug 20th 1918. Officer slightly wounded, 1 OR Killed & 10 OR slightly wounded. Officer slightly wounded. apparently no attempts to improve some hostile shelling on left Company front. Trench System very poor & apparently no attempts to improve.	
	20		Made for some time. Hostile shelling especially on right centre companies each of which shellshocked &c 40 OR 20 shellshocked. Hostile heavy Trench Mortars 12 hours 4 to 10.10 pm between guns 15 to 20 guns 3 OR Killed, 1 Officer & 40 OR wounded, one of whom died of wounds at cas. stn. T. I. Enemy Post Breused. at down on the 20th at Sheet 28 N.15.74 T.10,000 T. 16. 5.0040. with garrison of 6 Germans.	

WAR DIARY
or
INTELLIGENCE SUMMARY

Army Form C. 2118.

August 1918.

Place	Date	Hour	Summary of Events and Information	Remarks and references to Appendices
RIGHT BRIGADE SECTOR	20/21	3.0am	Strong patrols reconnoitred this hot (T.16.b.00-49) but in S our Trace. Enemy occupation beyond telephone wires. Other patrols on the front encountered enemy, other patrol crossed ZILLEBEKE LAKE but found this going difficult. 34.15 Div Patrols over Defence Scheme prepared.	E.
	21st		Quiet day with little shelling.	
	21/22nd		From 149 Division at 3.0am. Patrol again searched area about I.16.b.00.40. but work from Track Philadelphia & Road junction in I.21.d. Enemy positions. An Officers patrol in area of Railway & Road junction in I.21.d. came under mg fire at I.21.d.1.2.5. Other patrols from 5th The 9.	
VPRES	22nd		Daylight Patrol of 15 KHL Snipers under Ptc F.E. Snipers Sgt went out at 4.45am & proceeded to Gordon House in I.16.b searched area NW of same returning at 9.30am. Against trace of enemy outside huts. 9th patrol was not fired at. Day as a whole quiet with only an occasional sal-row I.15.d.9.2. & 42.ems & 5 blows m/s E side of YPRES/CHWY early part Spm 2 pt. Casualties 10 R killed.	
	22/23rd		Officers patrol again operated in area I.21.d. & was fired on by mg fire from several directions. Enemy appears to be located fairly close NE & outposts. Patrol proceeded as far as NIKERIE but only found 1 br well in the dark. Patrol on palm at I.12.6.9.2. & no other signs a Snipers post showing signs of fresh occupation Gordon House. 9-1/2 garra E Spt. The enemy. Patrol again searched Gordon House again & found no sign of posts. Enemy aircraft fairly active No Enemy Trestle. & were dropped about 10.50 pm near the FCOLF.	

WAR DIARY
or
INTELLIGENCE SUMMARY.

Army Form C. 2118.

AUGUST 1918

Place	Date	Hour	Summary of Events and Information	Remarks and references to Appendices
RIGHT BRIGADE SECTOR YPRES	22/23		Discovered late in the evening that 120 U.S. Regt. on our right were going to withdraw their posts until dusk 23rd, in view of possible enemy counter-preparation being put down on our line at Progress, had reported that an attack was expected by them. This left our right flank very much in the air, an officer was sent to American H.Qrs near KRUISSTRAAT F, but could only state that it was left post s which had hitherto interlocked with ours were that that their left posts which had hitherto interlocked with ours were about 300 yards almost directly in rear of our right post on this flank. 30/4 Machine guns were concentrated on this flank. Fairly quiet except for about 1 hour shelling at fairly rate of fire between 10 pm & 11 pm of junction of Right & Centre Companies. 1 pm 4 Suffolk Patrol (as on 22nd) proceeded with orders issuing M.K.H.2 cms. Daylight patrol carefully searched MORTED GRANGE which was carefully searched & S.P. GRANGE & reached nearly Patrol then proceeded to reconnaitre F. 8. HELLFIRE CORNER ROAD to ZWAAN, ZILLEBEKE - HELLFIRE CORNER ROAD. Saw no enemy movement & returned to our lines at about 10.0am & shall. Orders for relief by 11 Suffolks to-night issued early in the morning. Battalion going to be relieved by 11 Suffolks & relief in BRILLIA Camp, vacated by K.R.I. (29/4.2.a) who relieve Suffolks before rather can commence surf. But.	F

23rd

WAR DIARY or INTELLIGENCE SUMMARY

Army Form C. 2118.

August 1918

Place	Date	Hour	Summary of Events and Information	Remarks and references to Appendices
RIGHT BRIGADE SECTOR	23/24		Relief complete 12:45am 24th inst. But a long walk back to ORIHUIA Camp. Everybody in new Camp by 3:30am.	
ORIHUIA CAMP.	24th		All Companies & Headquarters bathed & supplied with clean clothing, by 5:0pm. Either at Siege Camp Baths, or Baths in A.30 central. Sheet 28. 1/40,000. No other parades.	
	25th		Parades from 8:30am - 12 noon. Close order Drill, Gas Drill, Musketry etc being carried out. Very large sick parades owing to an epidemic of diarrhoea throughout the Camp. Inter-Company football matches played in the afternoon. Camp half huts, half canvas, and very muddy. Huts being shelled two 6 inch guns exceedingly close, which, when not firing, where being shelled by the Hun with gas shells.	
	26th		Parades as yesterday, & more football matches. Many men at night, Company Commanders inspected opposite numbers of 11th H.L.I. Relieve 10th H.L.I. in support. Major W.J.N. preparations for Battalion Relieve on 26th inst.	
	27th		Parades until 11:30am. Preparations for Battalion Relieve keep's spare time of Battalion Mahanine Commanding 10th Battalion.	
	27/28		Relieved 10th Bn. H.L.I. in support. Two Companies (C+D) being forward between KRUISSTRAAT & YPRES — two Companies near Battn Headquarters at Bedstraw Castle. Relief complete by 10:30pm.	G.
SUPPORT.	28th		Quiet day. Quiet much doing. 1 Platoon from B Company working on Battalion Headquarters. 1 platoon from C Company on Brigade H.Q.	

WAR DIARY or INTELLIGENCE SUMMARY

Army Form C. 2118.

August 1916

Place	Date	Hour	Summary of Events and Information	Remarks and references to Appendices
RIGHT BRIGADE SECTOR	28th/29th		Enemy shelling for batteries caught C Company - one intensely shell killing 1 Officer - 2/Lt A.V. SMITH & wounding 30 O.R. 2/Lt SMITH was buried in his shelter, 14th H Bde relieving 34th Division leaving 43rd Bde in night. Subalterns so far retaliating.	
YPRES FRONT.	29th		Troops taken from B & C Companies working as usual from 6 a.m. – 12 noon.	
Support cont.	29th/30th		6 Platoons from A & B Company. 120 strong & 2 platoons St Eloi "A" Company - 50 strong working in the front line underparties from 9.30 pm - batt about 8 - 9.0 p.m. Rather heavy shelling of area 5 of Shrapnel Crossing about 1.30 a.m. Company Commanders visit H.Q. preparatory to relief tomorrow night. Arrangements made with 12th Suffolks regarding being relieved by them first.	
	30th		Usual platoons from B & C Companies working in front line. 6 Platoons from A & D Companies working in front line. 1 Officer & 140 O.R. dispatched to Corps 1st Camp at AUDRESSELLES for 14 days by Motor Buses. Relief orders for relief by 12th Suffolks relief of 10th HLI issued 2 platoons P.O. H
	30th/31st		4 C Companies working.	
	31st	12.30pm	Were received from Brigade reporting the enemy to have evacuated KENNEL area & possibly evacuating YPRES Front. Patrols from 10th HLI & Batt of 41st Bde are to investigate. Companies warned to be on night line sent out at noon to be ready to move at 15 minutes notice.	
		2.0pm	Major Millar sent to K.9.B Bde. arrangements made for disposal of Companies should necessity arise. No further information received until about 3.30 p.m., when all relief orders cancelled by Brigade, and	

Army Form C. 2118.

WAR DIARY
or
INTELLIGENCE SUMMARY.
(Erase heading not required.)

AUGUST 1918.

Place	Date	Hour	Summary of Events and Information	Remarks and references to Appendices
YPRES FRONT SUPPORT	31st		Normal procedure resumed. Rain at night hampers companies working on positions, but a quiet night. Enemy's trench mortars were on KEMMEL HILL. Dispatches from 10th H.L.I. on Right of the Sector came under fire from gordendahrs to enclose a similar distance on our S. of KILLETRAEK. Also reported enemy patrols from 4.15 Brigade suffered some casualties. Thus, does not appear that the enemy will retire on this front.	
	Cont.			

W. M. Malone
Major
Comdg 20th Middlesex Regt

August 31
1918

In the INTER-PLATOON COMPETITION the following were the marks awarded:

Unit	Judge	Cleanliness of Rifles - 7 marks	Cleanliness of men - 15 marks	Fitting Equipment - 7 marks	General Turn out - 15 marks	Steadiness in Ranks - 5 marks	Command - 10 marks	Handling of Arms - 20 marks	Drill - 20 marks	Total	Mean Total - 99 marks	Deduction	Result - 99 marks	
20th Middlesex Regt.	A Judge	5	13	7	14	4	9	17	17	86	81	Nil	81	1st Prize
	B Judge	4	13	4	11	3	10	16	15	76				
10th N.L.I.	A Judge	6	15	6	15	4	10	14	14	84	77.5	1.5*	76	2nd Prize
	B Judge	6	13	6	13	3	8	13	13	71				
12th Suffolk Regt.	A Judge	4	10	6	13	3	7	16	13	73	72	...	72	3rd Prize
	B Judge	4	9	6	10	4	8	15	16	72				

* No Lewis Gun on Parade

(sd) Colin Smee, Capt. & Adjt.
20th Middlesex Regt.

B.

SUPPLEMENTARY ORDERS TO ROUTINE ORDERS

Issue No: 28 d/- 5-8-18.

---

1. **RESULT OF BRIGADE TRANSPORT COMPETITION.**

Mess Cart.	1st.	12th Suffolks Regt.	135 Points.
	2nd.	20th Middx: Regt.	125 "
	3rd.	10th H.L.I.	119 "
Limbers	1st.	20th Middx: Regt.	175. "
	2nd.	12th Suffolk Regt.	167. "
	3rd.	10th H.L.I.	155. "
Cooker.	1st.	12th Suffolk Regt.	172 "
	2nd.	20th Middx: Regt.	130 "
	3rd.	10th H.L.I.	137 "
Pack Horse. *	1st.	12th Suffolk Regt.	(150 "
		20th Middx: Regt.	(150 "
	2nd.	10th H.L.I.	105 "
Rider.	1st.	12th Suffolk Regt.	160 "
	2nd.	20th Middx: Regt.	155 "
	3rd.	10th H L.I.	141 "

Prizes will be forwarded as early as possible.
* In the case of this tie - 5 francs will be given to each.

C. Wawbraw

20th Battalion, Middlesex Regiment.   Copy No: 11.
----------------ooOoo---------------

SECRET.

Operation Order No: 10.   11-8-18.
-----------------------   -------

Ref: Sheet 27a.N.E. 1/20,000.

1. The Battalion will move to LES MARAIS tomorrow August 12th, 1918.

2. TIMES.   Reveille:-   5.15.a.m.
               Sick Parade:-   5.30.a.m.
               Breakfast:-   6.a.m.
               Move off:-   7.30.a.m.

3. ORDER OF MARCH. H.Q., "A", "B", Drums, "C", "D" and Transport.
   The Head of the Column will pass "A" Companies Billet, N. of Headquarters at 7.30.a.m. The usual intervals will be maintained.

4. ROUTE. via MOULLE and SERQUES.

5. DRESS. Full Marching Order, less Haversacks and Greatcoats. Packs will be carried, but these will not be filled.i.e., Personal belongings and articles not immediately required by the men will be put in the Haversack, which, with the Greatcoats, will be carried by Lorry (see para 7)
   Water Bottles will be carried full.

6. ADVANCE PARTIES. 2/Lieutenant C.H.MONTAGUE and one N.C.O. per Company and Headquarters will proceed in advance to arrange Billets to be obtained from Area Commandant, WATTEN. These N.C.O's will report to 2/Lieut: MONTAGUE with Bicycles at Headquarters at 7.a.m.

7. BAGGAGE.
   Lorries to convey Baggage will be alloted, one per Company, "A" and "B" Companies first journey, "C" and "D" Companies second journey.
   O.C. Companies will arrange to have a small party, including men excused marching, etc., from their Companies to remain behind to load these Lorries and travel on them; also arrangements to guide the lorries to the respective Company Dumps. Lorries for "A" and "B" Companies will report at 8.a.m., Lorries for "C" and "D" Companies will report as soon as possible after completing the first journey. Baggage will be carried as follows:-
   All Companies:- Blankets rolled in 10's, Haversacks, Greatcoats,   Officers' Valises, Mobilization Stores, to be dumped at Company Headquarters at 7.a.m. (Haversacks and Greatcoats will be carried in Sandbags).
   in addition:-
   (1) "A" Companies Lorry will carry Band Blankets, Rifles, Packs, Greatcoats, etc., and Company Mess Kit to be at "A" Companies Dump by 7.a.m.
   (2) "B" Companies Lorry will carry Pioneers, Shoemakers and Tailors Stores and Kit, also Company Mess Kit to be at "B" Companies Dump by 7.a.m.
   (3) "C" Companies Lorry will carry the remainder of H.Q. Blankets, Haversacks, etc., to be at "C" Companies Dump by 7.a.m.
   (4) "D" Companies Lorry will carry the Transport Blankets, Greatcoats, etc., to be at "D" Companies Dump at 7.a.m.
   Headquarters Officers' Valises, Orderly Room and Canteen Stores, H.Q., "C" and "D" Companies Mess Kits will be dumped in H.Q. Yard at 7.a.m. to be loaded by Officers' Servants on to 1 G.S. Wagon and Mess Cart.

                                        Continued.

Operation Order No: 10 (Sheet 2)

---

8. **DINNERS.** Dinners will be served in new Area.
   Headquarters will hand over rations for dinners and teas in proportion to "A" and "B" Companies and will feed from the cookers of those Companies. Transport will act similarly with "C" and "D" Companies.

9. **DISCIPLINE.** Only one man will march behind each vehicle, except in the case of cookers, where 2 cooks will march behind each cooker. Any men surplus to one man per vehicle will march under an N.C.O., as a formed body in rear of Transport.

10. **REAR PARTY.** O.C. "D" Company will detail a party of one Officer and 12 other ranks to march in rear of the column.

11. **O.C. COMPANIES,** immediately on arrival, will inform Orderly Room of the number of men who fell out on the line of march.

12. **O.C. ADVANCE PARTY** will make any arrangements possible to get Baths at LES MARAIS after the troops arrive. O.C. Companies must be prepared to send their men to the Baths at short notice.

                               (sd) COLIN SHEE, Captain & Adjt:
                               20th Battalion Middlesex Regiment.

DISTRIBUTION.

Copy No:		
"	1	"A" Company.
"	2	"B" Company.
"	3	"C" Company.
"	4	"D" Company.
"	5	Second in Command.
"	6	Adjutant.
"	7	Quartermaster.
"	8	Transport Officer.
"	9	2/Lieutenant C.H. MONTAGUE.
"	10	R.S.M.
"	11	War Diary.
"	12	File.

20th Bn Middlesex Regt. No 12.

Secret.   12-8-18.
       Operation Order No 11.
Ref Sheets { 27A S.E 1/20,000
           { 27.   1/40,000.

1. The Battalion will move tomorrow to
LEDERZEELE via St MOMELIN.

2. Times.   Reveille   5.0 am
             Sick parade 5.15 am
             Breakfast   5.45 am.

3. Order of March. H.Q. B.C. Drums
D.A. Transport. Head of the column
will cross the bridge by Headquarters.
at 7.0. am.

4. Dress. As for today. Waterproof
sheets to be carried inside the
pack.

5. Advance parties. Usual advance
parties will report to 2/Lt Montague
at 6-30 am with bicycles at H.Q.
Billets will be obtained from Area Comd
LEDERZEELE. Tents are available on demand
as substitutes for Officers' billets.

2

6. Baggage:
As laid down in para 7 of O.O. No 10 will be dumped at each Coy H.Q. The conveyance of this baggage will be carried out in accordance with above para in O.O No 10, each Coy providing a loading party of men excused marching. Baggage tomorrow will be dumped at Coy H.Q.s by 6.30 am and lorries will report to each Coy at this time. Lieut & QM Barker will be in charge of the lorries and travel with them. O.C. Coys will detail a N.C.O. or man to be responsible for their lorry load of baggage.

Mess Cart will collect all mess kit only at 6-30 am.

H.Q Officers' valises & Room stores, etc. will be collected at H.Q by G.S. wagon at 6.30 am.

7. Meals. H.Q & Transport meals will be as for today (Aug 12th)

8. Supplies. on Aug 13th will be delivered to Area Comdt's office at LEDERZEELE at 6 pm at which time the QM will have a guide

3

at the above place to guide the lorry to the Battalion. Mail will be delivered with supplies.

9. Sick will be collected by 43rd F.A. at 6 a.m.

10. OC Rear Company will detail the usual rear party.

11. Attention is drawn to paras. 9 & 11 of O.O. No 10.

(Sgd) Colin Smee Capt Adj
20th Middlesex Regiment

Distribution.

Copy No	1	OC "A" Coy
"	2	" "B" "
"	3	" "C" "
"	4	" "D" "
"	5	Second in Command
"	6	Adjutant.
"	7	Quartermaster
"	8	Transport Officer
"	9	2/Lt Montague
"	10	Lieut & QM Barker
"	11	RSM
"	12	War Diary
"	13	File

20th Battalion Middlesex Regiment.

C2 Copy No: 14.
(War Diary)

SECRET

Operation Order No: 12.   13-8-18.

DUTIES for August 14th:-

   Orderly Officer:- 2/Lieutenant G.E.Pledger.
   Company for duties:- "C"

   Reveille:- 5.a.m.
   Sick Parade:- 5.15.a.m.
   Breakfast:- 5.45.a.m.
   Move off:- 7.30.a.m.

Ref: Sheet 27, 1/40,000.
HAZEBROUCK 5.a.

1. The Battalion will move to ESQUELBECQ, tomorrow, August 14th, via RUBROUCK.

2. ORDER OF MARCH. H.Q., "C", "D", Drums, "A", "B", Transport. Head of column to pass the road junction E of Church (C.25.b.20.95 - Sheet 27) at 7.30.am.

3. ADVANCE PARTIES, as usual, will report to 2/Lieutenant C.H. MONTAGUE at Headquarters at 7.am. Billets will be obtained from the Town Major, ESQUELBECQ. Tents can be obtained if required.

4. BAGGAGE. Arrangements for conveyance of baggage, loading parties, etc, will be the same as in Operation Order No: 11. Lorries will report at Company H.Qrs: at 7.am. Lieut: & Q.M. W.F.BARKER will be in charge of the Lorries. The G.S.Wagon and Mess Cart will report to Headquarters at 7.a.m.

5. SUPPLIES. On August 14th will be delivered to 43rd Brigade H.Q. (in ESQUELBECQ) at 6.p.m. The Quartermaster will arrange a guide to meet the lorries there at this time. Mails will be delivered by the Supply Lorries. This arrangement will hold for the successive days of the march.

6. Attention is drawn to paras: 4, 7, 9, 10, and 11 of O.O. No: 11.

7. The Battalion will move to DROGLANDT Area on August 15th and remain there until August 17th, when it will move to the PROVEN Area.

   (sd) COLIN SIMS, Captain & Adjutant,
   20th Battalion Middlesex Regiment.

DISTRIBUTION:-

Copy No: 1	"A" Company.	Copy No: 9	Medical Officer.
" 2	"B" Company,	" 10	2/Lieut: MONTAGUE.
" 3	"C" Company,	" 11	Lewis Gun Officer.
" 4	"D" Company,	" 12	Lt & Q.M. BARKER.
" 5	Second i/Command.	" 13	R.S.M.
" 6	Adjutant,	" 14	War Diary.
" 7	Quartermaster.	" 15	File.
" 8	Transport Officer.		

20th Battalion Middlesex Regiment.

Secret.

Operation Order No 13.

C3
Copy No 14
14/8/18.

DUTIES for August 15th:-

    Orderly Officer:- Lieutenant H.A.Stearn.
    Company for duties:- "D"

    Reveille:- 5. a.m.
    Sick Parade:- 5-15. a.m.
    Breakfast:- 5.45. a.m.
    Move off:- 7.0. a.m.

Ref. Sheet 27, 1/40,000
HAZEBROUCK 5.a.

1. The Battalion will move to Area N.E. of DROGLANDT, (Sheet 27,E,23,c and E,27,a,c,& d.) to-morrow August 15th via WORMHOUDT and HERZEELE.

2. ORDER OF MARCH H.Q., "B", "A", Drums, "D", "C", Transport. Head of the column to pass the cross roads at "C" Company's Billets (Sheet 27 C 2,b, 30,30. HAZEBROUCK 2 F, 25,75.) at 7-0 a.m.

3. ADVANCE PARTIES as usual will report to 2/Lieut., C.H.Montague at H.Q. at 3-30 a.m. Billets to be obtained from Area Commdt at DROGLANDT, also tents if required.

4. BAGGAGE will be conveyed by Lorry as usual. Lt.& Q.M.W.F.Barker will be in charge of the Lorries. O.C.Companies will only allow 6 men from their Companies to ride on the lorries and these men must be excused marching by the Medical Officer on to-morrow's sick parade; it is not necessary to send any other personnel on the lorries other than those excused marching. Lorries will report at Company dumps at 3.30. a.m.
The Mess Cart and G.S.Wagon will report at H.Q. at 3-30 a.m.

5. SUPPLIES Para.5 of O.O.No 12 is cancelled. Ration Lorries will report at Area Commandants Office DROGLANDT at 5. p.m.
The Quartermaster will arrange a guide to be there at this time.

6. WATER CART Refilling point is at WATOU.

7. MEALS H.Q. and Transport will in future arrange the cooking of their own meals on arrival.

8. Attention is drawn to paras 4, 9, 10, & 11 of O.O. No 11.

9. The Battalion will remain in DROGLANDT on August 16th and move on August 17th under orders to be issued later.

    (Sgd) COLIN SHEE Captain &
    Adjutant
    20th Bn. Middlesex Regiment.

DISTRIBUTION:-
Copy No. 1. O.C. "A" Company
" " 2. O.C. "B" Company
" " 3. O.C. "C" Company
" " 4. O.C. "D" Company
" " 5. Second in Command
" " 6. Adjutant
" " 7. Transport Officer
" " 8. Quartermaster.

Copy No 9. Medical Officer
" " 10. 2/Lieut,C.H.Montague
" " 11. 2/Lieut,R.J.Lucas
" " 12. Lt.& Q.M.W.F.Barker
" " 13. R. S. M.
" " 14. War Diary.
" " 15. File.

20th Battalion, Middlesex Regiment.

C4. War Diary

Copy No: 4

SECRET.

Operation Order No: 14.   16-8-18.

Ref: Sheet 27. 1/40,000.
HAZEBROUCK 5.a.

Duties for Aug: 17th:-

Orderly Officer:- 2/Lieut: E.P. Burman.
Company for duties:- "B"

Reveille:-   5. a.m.
Sick Parade:- 5.15. am.
Breakfast:-   5.45. am.

1. The Battalion will move to PROVEN Area tomorrow Aug 17th.

2. ORDER OF MARCH. H.Q., "A", "B", Drums, "D", "C", Transport.
    Head of column to pass "A" Companies billets on DROGLANDT - WATOU Road at 7.a.m. Dress as usual.

3. Route - WATOU - E.22.b.6.2. to billets.

4. ADVANCE PARTIES. Usual advance parties will report to
    2/Lieutenant C.H. MONTAGUE at 6.30.a.m. at Headquarters.
    Billets will be obtained from Area Commandant, PROVEN, F.13.b.8.8. Approximate billeting areas are
        F.14.a.4.3.   PIGEON.H.Q.
        F.8.c.1.3.   PRESTWICK.
        F.7.d.7.5.   MC LEAN.

5. TENTS. All tents will be struck and dumped at a convenient spot near a road for Lorries to collect and convey to Area Commandant at DROGLANDT, under the supervision of Lieut<u>n</u> & Q.M. BARKER, who will obtain a receipt for same. 37 tents were drawn from Area Commandant.

6. BAGGAGE, as usual, will be dumped at Company Headquarters by 6.30.a.m. and conveyed by Lorry under orders of Lieut: & Q.M. Barker. Baggage Wagon and Mess Cart will report to Headquarters at 6.30.a.m., at which time all baggage will be ready for loading.

7. Supplies for consumption 18th instant will be delivered tomorrow evening.

8. SICK will be collected one hour before moving off.

9. EAST of PROVEN- POPERINGHE Road, all movement will be by platoons at 100 yards intervals.

10. On arrival in the New Area, Training will be carried out in Patrol work and Gas drill.

(sd) COLIN SHEE, Capt: & Adjt:
20th Battalion Middlesex Regt.

DISTRIBUTION:-

As for Operation Order No: 13.

C5

20th Battalion Middlesex Regiment.   Copy No: 12

SECRET.   Operation Order No: 15.   17-8-18.

Ref: Sheet 27. 1/40,000.
     Sheet 28. 1/40,000.
     Hazebrouck 5.a.

1. The Battalion, less Transport, will move by train tomorrow to Area N. of VLAMERTINGHE.

2. ENTRAINING. The Battalion will entrain at PUGWASH - 27/E.6.b.5.7. at 8.30.a.m., as follows:-

   1st Train. 10 trucks - 30 per truck. "D" COMPANY and ½ "C" COMPANY.

   2nd Train. 10 trucks - 30 per truck. "B" COMPANY and ½ "C" COMPANY and 1 Platoon "A" COY.

   3rd Train. 9 trucks - 30 per truck. "A" COMPANY less 1 Platoon plus H.Qrs:

   Companies will leave camps at 7.30.a.m. to arrive at PUGWASH at 8.15.a.m. Companies will detrain at 28/B.27.d.2.2., and march to camp at 28/B.27.a.5.5. - SIEGE CAMP - under the Senior officer in charge of the train.

3. DRESS. Troops will entrain in FULL MARCHING ORDER, with Haversacks and Greatcoats.

4. SUPPLIES for consumption 19th instant will be delivered in new camp tomorrow.

5. TRANSPORT will move by march route to Camp at 28/C.4.c.4.9. leaving present camp at 8.30.a.m. The Battalion Transport Officer will allot camps in detail on arrival.

6. COOKERS AND WATER CARTS, will proceed to SIEGE CAMP under a N.C.O. and orders to be issued by the Transport Officer.

7. BAGGAGE.
   1. Blankets will be rolled in tens, labelled and stacked at Transport Lines before leaving camp, and will be carried to new transport lines by Baggage wagons.
   2. One Lorry will be retained for conveying Officers Valises, Mess Kit and Orderly Room Stores to SIEGE CAMP. This Lorry will be under the charge of 2/Lieut: R.J.LUCAS and will collect this baggage, which will be dumped at Companies Lines, as near to the road as possible by 7.a.m. One man per company will be left in charge of these dumps and a loading party of 1 N.C.O. and 4 men will be detailed from Headquarters by the R.S.M., to report to 2/Lieut: R.J.Lucas at Orderly Room at 7.a.m. This Lorry will be outside Headquarters at 7.a.m.

(sd) COLIN SHEE, Capt & Adjt:
20th Middlesex Regiment.

for Distribution see reverse.

DISTRIBUTION.

Copy No: 1. O.C. "A" Company.
"   2. O.C. "B" Company.
"   3. O.C. "C" Company.
"   4. O.C. "D" Company.
"   5. Second in Command.
"   6. Adjutant.
"   7. Quartermaster.
"   8. Transport Officer.
"   9. Medical Officer.
"   10. 2/Lieutenant R.J.LUCAS.
"   11. R. S. M.
"   12. War Diary.
"   13. File.

SECRET.　　　　WARNING OREDR and
　　　　　　　　ADMINISTRATIVE ORDERS.

Sheet 28.N.W.4. 1/10,000.
Sheet 28. 1/40,000.

1. The 43rd Brigade will relieve the 148th Brigade in the
   Right Sub-sector of 49th Division Sector on the
   night of August 19/20th.

2. The 20th Middlesex Regt. will relieve 4th Yorks & Lancs
   　　　　　　　　　　in Front Line (H.Q. at I.14.b.1.9.)
   12th Suffolk Regt: will relieve 4th K.O.Y.L.I., in
   　　　　　　　　　　Support (H.Q. at H.11.b.8.3.)
   10th H.L.I., will relieve in Reserve (H.Q. at
   　　　　　　　　　　　Remain　　　　　H.2.a.6.8.)
   43rd T.M.B. will relieve 148 T.M.B.

3. DISPOSITIONS.　"A" Company in Left Sub-sector.
   　　　　　　　　"B" Company in Centre　-do-
   　　　　　　　　"C" Company in Right　 -do-
   　　　　　　　　"D" Company in Reserve.

4. MOVE ORDERS will be issued later.

5. GUIDES, will be provided by 148th Infantry Brigade at
   a time and place to be notified later, on the
   following scale:-
   　　　2 for Battalion Headquarters.
   　　　1 per Company Headquarters.
   　　　1 per Platoon.

6. ADVANCE PARTIES. The following Advance Parties will proceed
   up the line to take over Trench Stores, Programmes of
   Work, Defence Schemes, Maps, Photographs, etc., tomorrow
   August 19th, leaving Camp at 7.30.a.m., under 2/Lieut:
   R.J.LUCAS and meeting a guide from 148th Brigade at a
   time and place to be notified later.
   　　　2/Lieutenant R.J.Lucas to Battalion Headquarters.
   　　　Signallers:- 2 per Battn: H.Q.　) to take
   　　　　　　　　　 1 per Company.　) over lines.
   　　　N.C.O's:-   1 per Company to take over Stores, etc.
   　　　Nos: 1 of L.G.Teams of
   　　　Front Line Platoons:- Total 10. - to take over
   　　　　　　　　　　important L.G.positions,etc.
   　　　　　TOTAL:- 21 All Ranks.

   　　Personnel from Companies will be given written
   chits stating the disposition of their respective
   platoons and companies when in the line. e.g. No: 1 of
   No: 9 Platoon L.G. Team will have a statement showing
   that his Company is "C" in the Right Sub-sector and
   his Platoon is No: 9 on the left (or right) of the
   Company Sector.

   　　　　　　　　(Continued)

Warning and Administrative Orders (Continued).

7. BAGGAGE.
   (a) SURPLUS BAGGAGE. Packs, Greatcoats, Officers' Valises, Surplus Mess Kit, Company Deed Boxes, Orderly Room Stores and all other Kit not taken up the line will be dumped at a spot near Headquarters, to be selected by the R.S.M., tomorrow, August 19th, at the following times:-   Packs & Greatcoats by 10. a. m.
   Officers' Valises and Surplus Mess
   Kit by 4. p. m.
   All other stores by 5. p. m.

   (b) Conveyance of baggage up the line will be as follows:-
   1 Limber per company will be allotted to carry Lewis Guns, Ammunition, Stretchers and Signalling equipment ONLY, as far as SHRAPNEL CROSSING: from there they will be man-handled. Cooking utensils, Mess Kit, H.Q's Kit, H.Q. Signalling Equipment and Orderly Room Box will be conveyed by Light Railway to Battalion Headquarters. Companies will send to Battn: H.Q. for Mess Kit carried for them in this manner, on completion of relief.
   Cooking utensils will be required as follows at Battalion Headquarters:-
   2 Boilers per Company - from Company Cookers.
   6 Camp Kettles from Headquarters.

8. PERSONNEL to be left with details is at present as follows:-

   COOKS.   2 per Company. Remaining 2 per Coy: will proceed up the line with Battn: H.Qrs.
   SIGNALLERS. 1 from Battalion Headquarters.
   PIONEERS. L/Cpl: & 3. Remainder (Sgt & 3) to proceed up the line.
   MESS CORPORAL and SERGEANT DRUMMER.
   H.Q. LEWIS GUNNERS. 4 (with 2 guns)

                    (Sd) COLIN SHEE, Captain & Adjt:
                         20th Battn: Middlesex Regiment.

D1 Copy Nº 12

20th Battalion Middlesex Regiment.

SECRET

Operation Order No: 16.   19-8-18.

Ref Map: Sheet 28. 1/40,000.

1. Reference para: 4 of Warning Order issued 18th instant, the
Battalion will move by rail from TROIS TOURS B.27.b.2.5.
to M.G. Farm Siding H.12.a.& b. by 3 trains as follows:-
"C" Company and 2 Platoons of "B" Company leave Camp at
8.10.p.m., entrain in No: 1 Train at 8.20.p.m.
"A" Company, and 2 Platoons and H.Qrs: of "B" Company
leave Camp at 8.15.p.m. and 8.20.p.m. respectively,
entrain in No: 2 Train at approx: 8.25.p.m.   "D" Company
and Headquarters leave Camp at 8.15.p.m. and 8.20.p.m.
respectively and entrain in No: 3 Train at approximately
8.30.p.m.

N.B. Each Train will consist of 9 trucks, holding 30 All
Ranks in each. No equipment will be taken off or rifles
left go of, during the journey. On arrival at detraining
station, Platoon Commanders will immediately detrain
their platoon and form them up at least 50 yards from
the railroad. Guides will meet their platoons at the
Railhead and platoons will march away without further
orders. Platoon Commanders will travel with their
platoons. Major W.W.MILNE, M.C., will travel on the
first train.

2. COMPLETION OF RELIEF will be wired to Battn: Headquarters
without delay, in code. The code word to be used will
be the name of the Company Commander concerned.

3. BAGGAGE. Company and Headquarter Lewis Guns, Signalling
Equipment and Company Stretchers will be taken on the
respective trains. Company and H.Qr: Mess Kit,
Cooking Utensils and Orderly Room Boxes also M.O's
Kit will be taken up to B.H.Q. by ration train from
TROIS TOURS in charge of Orderly Room Sergeant.
Company Mess Kit will be brought to Headquarters by
7.15.p.m.
2 men per company will go up with this kit by the
Ration Train. This party with baggage will leave camp at
7.30.p.m. and proceed to entraining station, load kit
on to the ration train for ST PIERRE CHURCH DUMP
(Right Batt: Headquarters) and travel up with it.
They will unload at this dump and wait for guides.
Companies will send parties to Battalion H.Q. for
their Kit as soon as possible after arriving in the
trenches and kit will be taken up to their
Headquarters by trolleys.

4. All Personnel being left behind will report to R.S.M.
at Headquarters at 6.p.m., unless other times have
been previously stated. This party will be
under the charge of 2/Lieutenant A.E.STABLER.

5. The following officers will remain behind and will report
to 2/Lieut: A.E.Stabler for instructions at 6.p.m.
2/Lieut: J.H.EWING.   2/Lieut: S.G.KILLICK,
2/Lieut: A.V.SMITH.

(sd) COLIN SHEE, Capt: & Adjt:
20th Bn: Middlesex Regiment.

DISTRIBUTION :-

Copy No: 1. O.C. "A" Company.
" 2. O.C. "B" Company.
" 3. O.C. "C" Company.
" 4. O.C. "D" Company.
" 5. Second in Command.
" 6. Adjutant.
" 7. Quartermaster.
" 8. Transport Officer.
" 9. Medical Officer.
" 10. 2/Lieutenant A.E.Stabler.
" 11. R.S.M.
" 12. War Diary.
" 13. File.

20th Middlesex Regiment.   RIGHT ~~SUB~~ BRIGADE SECTOR.
―――――――――――――――――   ―――――――――――――――――

SECRET.   PROVISIONAL DEFENCE SCHEME.   Ref: Sheet 28.N.W.4.
═══════   1/10,000.

1. THE BATTALION BOUNDARIES are:-
   ―――――――――――――――――――――――――

   SOUTHERN BATTALION BOUNDARY. YPRES-MENIN Railway
     (exclusive) from I.21.d.20.60. westward to
     I.20.a.10.95.
   NORTHERN BATTALION BOUNDARY. PIONEER TRACK (exclusive)
     from its junction with Front Line I.16.a.65.40. to
     its junction with SCHOOL ROAD at I.15.a.90.60.,
     thence MOAT LANE (exclusive) to its junction with
     YPRES DEFENCES about I.14.b.50.72.

2. DISPOSITIONS. The Battalion Front is held by 3 Companies, each
   ―――――――――――― with 2 Platoons in FRONT LINE and 2 Platoons in CLOSE
     SUPPORT LINE. Of the two close support platoons, one
     Platoon is at the disposal of the Company Commander for
     Counter-Attack purposes and one platoon is to be used
     as garrison for CLOSE SUPPORT LINE.
              The Support Company is distributed in SUPPORT
     LINE and is to be used under orders of the Battalion
     Commander.

3. PRINCIPLES OF DEFENCE. and ACTION IN CASE OF ATTACK.
   ――――――――――――――――――――――
   1. The FRONT LINE is the main line of resistance and is
      to be held to the last man and the last round.
   2. Every foot of ground is to be disputed in the event of
      an attack. Should the enemy penetrate any portion
      of the line, he is to be driven out by:-
        (a) Immediate Counter-attack by Support Platoon
            under direct orders from Company Commander.
        (b) Immediate Counter-attack by Support Company
            under orders of Battalion Commander.
        (c) Deliberate Counter-attack by Brigade or
            Divisional Reserves (preceded by Artillery
            preparation), if the penetration is so serious
            that a counter-attack by LOCAL RESERVES cannot
            be expected to restore the situation.
      In (a) the Company Commander and in (b) the Battalion
      Commander must decide whether to use his Support
      Platoon or Support Company as Stoppers or for
      Counter-attack. It is, as a rule, very little use
      launching a Counter-attack unless the enemy is held.
   3. In case of a rupture in the line to the South, it may
      be necessary for the Support Company to man the
      line of the ZILLEBEKE from I.15.d.0.2. to
      I.15.a.0.0., or in case of great urgency, for Centre
      Company to man the same line with its 2 Close
      Support Platoons.

4. COMMUNICATIONS.
   ―――――――――――――
      (a) By telephone to and from all Company Headquarters.
      (b) By Lamp or Disc to and from all Company Headquarters.
      (c) By Message Carrying Rockets to and from all Company
                                                    Headquarters.
      (d) By Pigeon from Right Company Headquarters and Battalion
                                                    Headquarters.
      (e) From Battalion to Brigade Headquarters, via Advanced
          Station by Telephone, Power Buzzer, Lamp, Message
          Carrying Rocket and Pigeons.

                                              P. T. O.

5. WORKING AND DETATCHED PARTIES.
    These Parties will come under orders of O.C. Sub-Sector in which they are working. O.C. Party will report as soon as possible to O.C. Sub-Sector the location of his party and await orders.

6. In the event of a hostile barrage being placed on any portion of the Battalion Front, the garrison of that part of the line will move forward 100 yards and occupy Shell-holes, and await events. The O.C. Patrolling Party on Battalion Front will at once move his patrol across to the threatened portion of front to protect the line. Should the enemy be attempting a raid, he will make every effort to intercept hostile raiding party advancing or returning to or from the raid.

7. Medical Aid Post is at Battalion Headquarters.

                    (sd) COLIN SHEE, Captain and Adjutant,
                        20th Battalion, Middlesex Regiment.

Distribution
All Companies.
(Left Brigade) Right Battalion
43rd Infantry Brigade
War Diary
Handing over File.
Office (2)

Addendum to
Provisional Defence Scheme
SECRET   Right Brigade Sector.

Ref: 5.2.
(a) Three definite platoon zones will be selected in the front line to be held permanently by 1 platoon in each case. These zones will be defended to the very last man. The remaining platoon per Company in the front line may be used as a manoeuvre platoon for the defence of front line.

(b) The same principles will be adopted with regard to the close support line. 1 per platoon per Company will be a permanent garrison to a selected defensive zone in the close support line whilst the remaining platoon is at the disposal of the Company Comdr for manoeuvre purposes for the defence of the Battalion front.

(c) Sketch map attached showing zones (Bde & Batn HQ only)

Col. Snell
Captain Adjutant
B/8/18   2o Bn Middx Regt

F to Come

Secret.   20th Middlesex Regiment.
              Operation Order No 17.
Ref: Sheet 28 A.II 1/20 000   Copy No. 14.
       28 A SW 1/20 000
_____

1. The Battalion will be relieved in the Right Bde Sector on the night Aug 20/21st 1918 by the 12th Suffolk Regt.

2. Relief will be carried out as follows:-
   A Coy 20th Mx will be relieved by
   D Coy 12th Suffolks.
   B Coy 20th Mx   —"—   —"—
   B Coy 12th Suffolk.
   C Coy 20th Mx   —"—   —"—
   A Coy 12th Suffolks
   D Coy 20th Mx   —"—   —"—
   C Coy 12th Suffolk.

3. Guides on the scale of 1 per platoon and 1 per Company HQ will be provided as follows

(a) For Right & Centre Companies
(A & B Companies 12th Suffolks)
Guides will be at junction
of LILLE & WARRINGTON Roads
(I 20, a 6.9) at 10.30 pm.
(b) For left Company (D Coy
12th Suffolks) guides will
be at junction of RAILWAY
& LILLE Road (I 14 c 7 8)
at 10.30 pm.
(c) No guides will be provided
for Support Company or
Battalion Headquarters.
* Guides will be in possession
of written chits stating
the platoons they are
to meet and the position
to which they are to guide
the in coming platoons.
4. All Trench Stores, including
full & empty water tins
will be handed over and
receipted lists obtained
which will be forwarded to

Orderly Room by 6pm aug 24th

5, Completion of Relief will be wired by code word of Company Commanders name. On completion of relief the Battalion will move into Divisional Reserve at ORILLA CAMP 28/H 2 a 6.7., moving into bilets vacated by 10th H.L.I.

Platoons will move at 100 yards distance via WARRINGTON Road – KRUISSTRAAT SHRAPNEL Crossing and hence to YLAMERTINGHE. One limber per Company for conveyance of Lewis Guns etc will be on the YPRES – YLAMERTINGHE Road 200x W. of GOLDFISH CHATEAU by 11.30 pm.

The Quartermaster will arrange for sufficient guides to be from the X roads at YLAMERTINGHE and the

4

Camp to direct Companies into the Camp. Guides to be in position by midnight.

6. The Quartermaster will arrange for an Officer from details to proceed to ORILLA CAMP and take over all stores and papers from 10th H.L.I by 2 pm 23rd inst.; that all blankets, Officers Valeises &c are taken to ORILLA CAMP and distributed; and that meals are ready for the men on arrival, and that 'O'room boxes, Band instruments and other requirements are taken to new Camp.

7. The Transport Officer will arrange for Limbers for Headquarters to be at I 8 b 10 80 S of MENIN GATE at 11.30 pm.

8. Of Companies will send their boilers and any mess kit that cannot be carried, to BHQ by returning Ration trucks which will bring up Suffolks Rations under D Companies pushing parties at the usual time. As much mess kit as possible must be carried.

9. Advance parties from Suffolk Regiment will report to Company H.Q. after 8 p.m.

10. Arrangements for Baths & Pay on 24th will be notified later.

11. Notification will be forwarded to O Room immediately on arrival in billets.

C W Small
Capt & Adjt
20th Middlesex Regt

23/8/18

Distribution
No 1 Copy to OC A Coy
2 —   B
3 —   C
4 —   D
5 —   Second in Command
6 —   Signals
7 —   Lewis Gun Officer
8 —   Medical Officer
9 —   Quartermaster
10 —   Transport Officer
11 —   8th Suffolks
12 —   10th H.L.I.
13 —   R.S.M.
14 —   War Diary ✓
15 —   File.

Ref O.O. No 17.

Ref para 3. One Officer per
Company will proceed to my H.Q.
hours as stated, with the
guides from his Company.

Ref para 5. Platoon Commanders
will carefully study the route
to be followed on the map so
as to avoid any confusion.

2/10/18   Capt & Adjutant
                 2nd Middlesex Regiment.

20th Battalion, Middlesex Regiment.   Copy No: 13

SECRET.   Operation Order No: 18.   26-8-18.

Ref: Sheet 28.N.W. 1/20,000.
     28.N.W.4. 1/10,000

1. The Battalion will relieve the 10th Bn: H.L.I., in Support to RIGHT BRIGADE SECTOR on night 27/28th August, 1918.

2. Relief will be carried out as follows:-
   "A" Coy: 20th Middlesex will relieve "C" Company H.L.I.
   "B" Coy: -do-   -do-   "B" Company H.L.I.
   "C" Coy: -do-   -do-   "A" Company H.L.I.
   "D" Coy: -do-   -do-   "D" Company H.L.I.

   Companies will move off as follows:- "D", "A", "C", "B", H.Q., at 7.15.p.m. by ½ platoons at 100 yards distance.

3. GUIDES, on the scale of 1 per platoon and Company H.Q., and 2 for Bn: H.Q. will be 200 yards West of SHRAPNEL CROSSING at 8.p.m. Platoons will close up on meeting guides, but will not halt.

4. 1 Limber per Company will be allotted for carriage of Lewis Guns, etc., and 1 Limber for Headquarters: in addition, 1 Limber with 20 full water-tins each for "A" and "D" Companies will proceed with "A" Company. All tins will be dumped at "A" Company Headquarters and "D" Company will send a party to draw from there. 1 Full Water Cart for the use of "B" and "C" Companies and Headquarters will proceed with H.Q. and remain in the new position, with the horses. All Transport will report at ORILLA Camp not later than 6.30.p.m.

5. ADVANCE PARTIES, of Signalling Officer and 2 N.C.O's from H.Q. 1 Officer, Company Gas N.C.O., 1 Runner, 1 Signaller per Company and 1 N.C.O. per platoon will proceed in advance, leaving camp at 2.p.m., to take over all trench stores, Work, Defence Schemes, etc., Receipted lists being forwarded to B.H.Q. by 10.a.m. August, 28th. Advance Parties will wear the haversack at the side, and not on the back.

6. Blankets and Packs will be dumped near the entrance to the Camp by Companies by 8.30.a.m. August 27th, together with Band Instruments, Surplus Signalling Stores, and Lewis Gun Equipment. Officers' Valises, and Surplus Mess Kit will be dumped at 4.p.m.

7. Battalion Headquarters will be at BOBSTAY CASTLE.

8. Relief complete will be wired by code word of Company Commander's Name.

                    (sd) COLIN SHEE, Capt: & Adjt:
                         20th Middlesex Regiment.

DISTRIBUTION.

No: 1 "A" Company,   No: 9 Quartermaster.
    2 "B" Company,   10 Transport Officer.
    3 "C" Company,   11 R.S.M.
    4 "D" Company.   12 O.C. 10th H.L.I.
    5 Second in Command.   13 War Diary.
    6 Adjutant,   14 File.
    7 Lewis Gun Officer.
    8 Signalling Officer.
    8a. Medical Officer.

20th Battalion Middlesex Regiment.

Copy No 14.

SECRET.   OPERATION ORDER No: 19.

31 AUG 1918

Ref Sheets 28.N.W. 1/20,000.
           28.N.W.4. 1/10,000.

A. 1. The Battalion will be relieved by the 12th Bn: Suffolk Regt.
      in SUPPORT on night 31st Aug/1st Sept.

   2. Relief will be as follows:-
      "A" Coy: Middlesex will be relieved by "A" Coy: Suffolk Rgt.
      "B" Coy: Middlesex will be relieved by "C" Coy: Suffolk Rgt.
      "C" Coy: Middlesex will be relieved by "B" Coy: Suffolk Rgt.
      "D" Coy: Middlesex will be relieved by "D" Coy: Suffolk Rgt.

   3. GUIDES for B&D Company Suffolk Regt to be at junction of KRUISSTRAAT Road and Warrington Rd at 8.35pm. For A&C Companies 12th Suffolks to be at Shrapnel Crossing at 8pm. No guides will be supplied for BHQ. All guides to be on the scale of 1 per Platoon + 1 per Coy HQrs. Each guide to be in possession of a written chit shewing the position for which he is acting as guide.

   4. ADVANCE PARTIES, from Suffolk Regt. will arrive during
      the day to take over trench stores, etc.

   5. COMPLETION OF RELIEF will be wired by code word of O.C.
      Companies name, followed by the word ONE.

B. 6. On completion of relief by Suffolk Regiment, the Battalion
      will relieve the H.L.I., in Right Brigade Sector.

   7. Relief will be as follows:-
      "A" Company, Middlesex will relieve "C" Coy: H.L.I., in
                                           Left Sub-Sector.
      "B" Company, Middlesex will relieve "B" Coy: H.L.I., in
                                           Centre Sub-Sector.
      "D" Company, Middlesex will relieve "A" Coy: H.L.I., in
                                           Right Sub-Sector.
      "C" Company, Middlesex will relieve "D" Coy: H.L.I., in
                                           Support.

   8. GUIDES. A Company will move via Railway, meeting guides at junction of Railway & Lille Rd at 10pm. B Company will move via Warrington Road meeting guides at junction of Warrington & Lille Roads at 10pm. 'D' Company will move via Warrington Road, meeting guides at same place & time as B Company. C Coy will move via 'Dead End' meeting guides here at 10pm. There will be no guides for BHQ. Guides will be on the scale of 1 per Platoon + 1 per Coy HQ. 1 NCO for Signal Stores.

   9. ADVANCE PARTIES, of 1 Officer, 1 Signaller and Gas N.C.O., 1 NCO for Signal Stores
      per Company, and 1 N.C.O. per Platoon and from Headquarters
      will proceed up in advance to take over all trench stores
      maps, defence and work schemes, etc. Receipted Trench
      Store Lists to be sent to Orderly Room with Intelligence
      Summary, morning of September 1st.

   10. RATIONS, for consumption Sept: 1st, will be sent up be
       train to LILLE GATE and will be pushed up to Companies
       positions by H.L.I. pushing parties. O.C. Companies will
       arrange for a responsible N.C.O. from the Advance Party lorry bus to Ypres
       to be at LILLE GATE at 8.50 p.m. to receive the rations
       from the Q.M.Sgts: who will accompany the train to
       LILLE GATE. This N.C.O. will take charge of the rations
       until the arrival of the Company.

   11. COMPLETION of this relief will be wired by code word of
       Company Commanders name, followed by the word TWO.

   12. The Water Cart, at present at Headquarters will return
       to Transport Lines as soon after dark as possible on
       August 31st.

P. T. O.

13. A limber for A & D Companies, and 1 limber for B & C Companies & HQ, will report at HQ "A" Company & Battalion HQrs respectively at 8.30pm to take back surplus cooking utensils, water tins & Medical Stores etc, which must be ready at the above places at the times stated.

14. O/C Details will arrange that the Drums personnel less the Sgt Drummer report to Bn HQrs not later than 8.30pm 31st August.

15. Messkit of B & C Companies & HQrs, O Room Stores etc will be loaded on two trucks at siding H 5 d 6 5 at about 7.30pm Aug 31st. These trucks will be taken to YPRES by a train passing about 8.30pm. Only one man from each of B & C Companies will remain with the trucks when loaded. Unloading party (to travel on trucks) will be detailed from HQrs. Arrangements will be made for C Company to push up 'B' Company's Mess Kit from YPRES on the Ration Trolleys.

Col. Smee
Captain and Adjutant,
20th Battn: Middlesex Regiment.

DISTRIBUTION:-

Copy No: 1   "A" Company.
2   "B" Company.
3   "C" Company.
4   "D" Company.
5   Adjutant.
6   Second in Command.
7   Signal Officer.
8   Lewis Gun Officer.
9   A/R. S. M.
10   10th H. L. I.
11   12th Suffolk Regt.
12   Quartermaster.
13   Transport Officer.
14   War Diary. ✓
15   File.
16   MO
17   O/C Details

WAR DIARY
20th (S) Bn Middlesex Regt.

September 1918.

Army Form C. 2118.

WAR DIARY
or
INTELLIGENCE SUMMARY.

(Erase heading not required.)

Place	Date	Hour	Summary of Events and Information	Remarks and references to Appendices

Instructions regarding War Diaries and Intelligence Summaries are contained in F. S. Regs., Part II. and the Staff Manual respectively. Title pages will be prepared in manuscript.

WAR DIARY or INTELLIGENCE SUMMARY

Army Form C. 2118.

SEPTEMBER 1918

Place	Date	Hour	Summary of Events and Information	Remarks and references to Appendices
YORES FRONT	1/9/18		Last day in Support. Tours this changes from 4 to 5 days. Relieved 14/T in front line having first been relieved by 12th Suffolks. 1st Relief complete 10.45pm 2nd Relief (see August W.D.) front line complete 12.45 am.	H
Front line	2nd		Usual Trench Work & Patrols at night; moon hampers by pitch blackness.	
	3rd		Daylight Patrols. No information obtained. Usual work during Patrols.	
	4th		Usual Trench Work. MANOR FARM strafed in the afternoon as though it should be walking Certain machine guns & posts. As usual no firing took place from there a rod during the night; if at any machine gun fires took place for two minutes, light T.M. put up to the artillery would concentrate on it for 2 minutes. No M.G. fire however at all.	
	5th		Repeated procedure with MANOR FARM, this MG fire from Hermal. Daylight Patrols. Strains useful for via road GORDON HOUSE, there. Daylight Patrols NOT so successful, absolutely no area to CAVALRY ROAD. Night Patrols usefully angled by observing rifle flashes. An officer & 10 OR accidentally met the French piled & flashed by a working party. 9 OR, back in the French bayonets: also 1 German in a working party patrol on scratched with a bayonet. New enemy post located by above patrol on CAVALRY ROAD about halfway between GORDON HOUSE & HEMMINGTON READ. Assembly fired first not 19 team which 3 places & the rest made the rest nished old gun lost.	

Army Form C. 2118.

WAR DIARY
or
INTELLIGENCE SUMMARY.
(Erase heading not required.)

September 1918

Place	Date	Hour	Summary of Events and Information	Remarks and references to Appendices
YPRES Rest fund.	6th		Nothing to report about 5pm then reported that proper night operations under orders on Kething Blue Post Farm, Damagements immediate. Strong patrol to MANOR FARM. Subsidiary TM's, Rifle Grenadier along the Railway & 4 guns on the S. Bank 67 1st Lahore Infantry, to operate. Cancelled about 4.45pm, as unit other in Reserve. Blue Post Fasta.	A.
	6/7th		Relieved by 1/5th Suffolks – Track to Reserve in STRIWITL 10:- long rest owing to darkness & mist.	
RESERVE BILLITCAMP.	7th 8th		Some rain in b very wet. Work as keep as far as possible to collect Material from derelict camps, which everybody seems to foster. Very wet.	
	9th		Baths for the Battalion at SARATOGA & SIEGE Camps. Very wet.	
	10th		Some training 2IE work on Camp. Very wet. Battalion Concert 11C Evening.	
	11th		Some training & preparing to move to Support. Continue work on Camp under difficulties of strong wind & heavy rain.	B.

WAR DIARY or INTELLIGENCE SUMMARY

Army Form C. 2118.

September 1918.

Place	Date	Hour	Summary of Events and Information	Remarks and references to Appendices
YPRES Support Line	12th		In Support; dispositions as before. 1 Platoon furnishes rat Company orderlies on Brigade Battalion Headquarters & Aircraft Guard; this being inside the late Mess Kitchen at Battn Headquarters. Much rain & high wind. 7 Platoons out at night working in Support line in forward area. Platoons working in near Bn Headquarters had a Normal day. An extra Platoon working to also a small room being built room for Trench feet treatment at Battalion Headquarters/Sh the same purpose.	
	13th		No work to-night.	
	13th/14th		Early Morning, orders received that Battalion was moving on the night 14/15/15/16 in Motor Buses except in the case of D Company which was but that no unit was coming in except 1/5th Yorkshire Dragoons attached to the being relieved by him from 1/5th Yorkshire Dragoons at Suicide Corner & he conveys to Blue Grass, leaving Battalion was to entrain to School Camp at 27/4.3.c.5.5. There were 10 Shut 27/ F. 28.c.1.9 & then proceed to School Camp at 10 pm. Transport moving on separate orders to two trains of 13 trucks each at 10 pm. Transport moving on separate orders during the day, the whole Brigade being similarly. 1 Platoon working all day on Cable Trench near the two Bde Signal Offices.	C
	14th		As no one was actually relieving 3 Company's & 4 Bn HQ some question as to disposal of P.D.D... stores but finally decided that 4 Dragoons would see up 2 men to each position being evacuated	

Place	Date	Hour	Summary of Events and Information	Remarks and references to Appendices
YPRES	14/9/15		Rest of Battalion present entraining point at 10.0pm but in 2 trains. 1st train arrived about 10.30pm & had only 7 trucks; it then being discovered that this would be 4 trains, 2 of trucks, & 2 of 6 trucks! By dint of much hardwork on the part of entraining officers, the whole battalion eventually accommodated in 3 trains of 21 trucks altogether, & last train departed about 11.0pm. A cold night & some little rain. Trains eventually ran practically at walking pace. Arrived at the camp about 1.30-2.0am. Accommodation for S/S be Nissen huts & tents. There were all squashed as the tents were, as usual unfit for habitation. Unfortunately no groundsheets or spades for men on arrival as the Transport which was 15 Horse-wagons & strong(?) horses on arrival. The transport unit this new camp during the day, but [illegible] unknown orders after the 2nd journey, causing great inconvenience & 9 x tea made for 1st line Horse-transport.	
SCHOOL CAMP Shal 27 L/3 G.S.S.	15/9/15		Reveille 9.30am. Breakfast by 11.0am. A warm day mostly spent in cleaning up. Visited by Brig. Genl during the afternoon.	
	16/9		Training carried on until all day. A fair amount of ground offering possibilities of some useful work being carried out.	

WAR DIARY
INTELLIGENCE SUMMARY.

Army Form G. 2118.

September 1918.

Place	Date	Hour	Summary of Events and Information	Remarks and references to Appendices
SCHOOL CAMP Sh.27 H2 c 5.5	17th		Training with Range work all day. Evening practice attack carried out by all Companies. 2 Companies at a time. Lectures to under Officers.	
	18th		Cases shown sign of commonsense which was gratifying. Similar training. Attack practice again carried out, but with Stores & Smoke bombs to represent damage. Troops appear to be unkeeled tired hard to best of their ability.	
	19th		Similar training. Attack again carried out with Enemy hy Posts &c dealt with. This proved rather a failure the posts being rather too close to the First Objective.	
	20th		Some training; preparation for move forward, the Division relieving 35th Division in the line. 43 Bde taking over from park Sp 42nd Brigade. Battalion marched out at 7.0 pm to DOMINION CAMP Shs.28.G.23b & 9.24 a.	D.
DOMINION Camp Shs 28.G.23.b G.24.a.			Arrived in camp about 9.30 pm. Accommodated in huts. Transport at Shs.28. G.23.c.	

WAR DIARY or INTELLIGENCE SUMMARY

Army Form C. 2118.

September 1918.

Place	Date	Hour	Summary of Events and Information	Remarks and references to Appendices
DOMINION Camp.	21st		Day spent in cleaning up and training in huts. No movement allowed by day.	
Sheet 28 G3 d. G.S.W.	22nd		Short period spent in training under cover. Orders for two Coys to relieve two Coys of HLT on night 22/23rd. Training and games. Orders for relief cancelled.	
	23rd		Systems of night drill, training as usual. One platoon of A. Coy. sent forward from aeroplanes about midnight.	
	24th		Equipped for an offensive, but to act as a working half. Orders received for above mentioned relief, to be carried out night 25/6. Band practised all day.	
	25th		Training by 2 Coys in huts owing to wet. Cat P Coys carried out relief. Rain continued. Practice. Two Companies 12 Stos in Camps vacated by our Companies.	E.
DOMINION Camp. Sheet 28 G3 b. G.S.W.	26th		Preparing for move in to Forward area of remainder of Battalion & 2 Companies of 12th Suffolks. Equipping men with extra Explosives & R.E. Stores for active operations	F.

Army Form C. 2118.

WAR DIARY
or
INTELLIGENCE SUMMARY.
(Erase heading not required.)

September 1918.

Place	Date	Hour	Summary of Events and Information	Remarks and references to Appendices
CANAL SECTOR	27th	10:00am	Conference of Company Commanders. Orders for the attack on S side of YPRES COMINES Canal by the Battalion (with 11th Sh. R. Hnde on the Canal & 10th H.L.I. in reserve, A & B Coy on right, & C & D Bde in reserve) on morning of Sept 28th discussed & all arrangements made. Operation Orders issued - watches synchronised & zero hour 5:30am 28th inst. notified to Companies.	G
	28th	2:30am	Bn Headquarters moved up to Left Company front line. Headquarters Companies in position in assembly lines at 5:00am.	
		5:30am	Barrage commenced. Enemy rifle slight, but hit Battalion HQ shelter in the first few minutes. No casualties.	
		6:15am	No information having been received from Companies & Snipers set up from HQ to try & find out situation.	
		7:20am	Several parties of prisoners (8 or 10 in a batch, as far as our wounded seen coming back. Major (Garnish & 2/Lt MONTAGUE sent up to establish An HQ at NORFOLK Lodge in Canal Bank.	
		7:45am	Information from Right Company 1st Objective that First Objective taken 6:45am with slight casualties, but much opposition. Units are on thought to be apparently in position after attack & ground gained. Battalion HQ moved up to tunnel in Canal Bank near NORFOLK Lodge.	
		8:30am	No further information having been received.	
		9:00am	Report timed 8:20am from L/Cpl KEATING 9/ Company. Company somewhat disorganised, but digging in apparently on the 1st objective. (Capt J. K KEATING)	

WAR DIARY
or
INTELLIGENCE SUMMARY
(Erase heading not required.)

Army Form C. 2118.

September 1918.

Place	Date	Hour	Summary of Events and Information	Remarks and references to Appendices
Canal Sector	28th	11:15 am	Information (rumour) from Right Company on Final Objective (C Company) that final objective has been taken, but not in touch with right. That patrols sent out try to get touch. Ran in 16 enemy MG posts. Casualties about 12.	
		12:45 pm	Left Company on Final Objective (D Company) reports attained 9:20 am, states final objective taken. Casualties about 12, so about 30 prisoners taken. Thus all positions taken, consolidation being carried on. Companies in touch with one another & Left Battalion well up. Since touch with right Battalion not yet gained. Casualties slightly & numerous rests or numbers of prisoners taken.	
		1:45 pm	Message from Brigade states 41st Division on the left (N.S. Canal) were ordered at about 10:00 am to attack M. 4. T. of Canal.	
		1:10 pm	2/Lt MONTAGUE sent to endeavour to find HQ of WILTS, has gone as touch not yet obtained except for a few stragglers with our A Company. No sign has been seen of them since zero hour.	
		2:00 pm	Report from 2/Lt MONTAGUE saying a WILTS officer informs him, we (Middlesex) have a post in front of FRIST FARM. No officer of WILTS is NP with his battalion & does not know where it is. / Situation on the right still obscure, no sign of the WILTS is to

WAR DIARY
INTELLIGENCE SUMMARY.

Army Form C. 2118.

September 1918.

Place	Date	Hour	Summary of Events and Information	Remarks and references to Appendices
Canal Sector	20th	2.30pm	Wire from Brigade sending GOC Division & GOC Brigade's congratulations from on our success. Patrols pushed out to try & find out if enemy is retiring. Hidden areas in front of left Coy (D) was reported firing & B Company to hypothesis established on the high ground & E & F STAGGERS LANE. OC D Company secured this position against any assembly for a counterattack. Touch established on my front & its right flank with the WILTS. Two platoons of H.I moved up to assist strong Von Linie in General.	H
		2.45pm	OC A Company right support Company reports Patrol is established a post in El KHOT FARM. Firing continued at WILTS.	
		4.45pm	A Company report being in touch with WILTS by a post 50 yards N.E. of RUINED FARM. But front line Company not yet in touch. Patrols report no sign of enemy with the exception of a few stragglers. No sign of 31st Division, although expected 15 March 1st Objectives (28/ R.13.central & P.8.d central) at about 4.30pm	
	*		Report from Brigade that Division the right held at houstraete FARM. 08.c.00.35	
		4.30pm	Orders issued for reorganization of the Line & forming of a defensive right flank, with 1 platoon of H.I between C Co's right & A Co's right.	I
	*		Quiet night. Patrols out but restricted to 300 yards advance in view of 11ers	

Army Form C. 2118.

WAR DIARY
or
INTELLIGENCE SUMMARY.
(Erase heading not required.)

September 1918.

Instructions regarding War Diaries and Intelligence Summaries are contained in F. S. Regs., Part II. and the Staff Manual respectively. Title pages will be prepared in manuscript.

Place	Date	Hour	Summary of Events and Information	Remarks and references to Appendices
Canal Sector	28th		No movement of 41 Division on ULC left.	
	29th	4:10 am	Orders received from Brigade that 34th Division is moving eastward at 5:30am to join up with 41st Division whose right is on the Canal at P13 central, & that 14th Divn conforming with movement of 34th Division is to clear ground up to the Canal at this point. Orders sent to Companies to move & conform with the right.	
		10am	C Company report that patrol gained touch at southern end of DAMSTRASSE with 34th Division without encountering WLTS.	J.J.
		12:30pm	C & D Companies in new positions 12:30pm	
		1:30pm	A Company in new position 12:30pm	
		2:0pm	Bn Headquarters advanced to WHITE CHATEAU. Patrols out in front of battalion reported 'cut out' by joining of 41st & 34th Divisions at about 8:0pm. 5 Field guns located.	
		4:45pm	Orders received for withdrawal return to Dickie Bush Area. Last Company moved at 6:30pm & marched to Smythe Camp. Raining in torrents & accommodation extraordinarily bad & insufficient. Last Company arrived about 4:0am.	
Smythe Camp	30th		Raining, impossible to clean up, no tarps available, but troops very cheerful.	

W. Wincken Major
Comdg 20th Bn Middlesex Regt.

Army Form C. 2118.

WAR DIARY
or
INTELLIGENCE SUMMARY.
(Erase heading not required.)

Summary of Events and Information

Summary of Prisoners & War Material taken during Operation 28/29/15

Prisoners. 210 approx. Guns. 1 – 3" 5. 77m. T.M's. 2. M.Gs 10-12 light 4 heavy.

Casualties. Killed 13. O.R. wounded 2 off. 58 O.R. missing. 6.

Strength of Battalion in the attack. 16 Officers & 545 O.R's.

W. M. Mulu
Major
Comdg 20th Middlesex Regt.

War Diary

— Battalion, Middlesex Regiment.

Copy No: 14

SECRET.

Operation Order No: 20.

A

Ref: Sheet:
28.N.W. 1/40,000

1. The Battalion will be relieved by the — Bn: Suffolk Regt., on the night Sept 6/7th: on completion of relief the Battalion will be in Brigade Reserve at ORILLA Camp.

2. Order of relief as follows:-
   "A" Coy: Middlesex will be relieved by "D" Coy: Suffolks.
   "B" Coy: Middlesex   "   "   "   " "B" Coy: Suffolks.
   "D" Coy: Middlesex   "   "   "   " "C" Coy: Suffolks.
   "C" Coy: Middlesex   "   "   "   " "A" Coy: Suffolks.

3. Completion of relief will be wired by code word of Company Commander's name.

4. GUIDES will be provided for "A" & "C" Companies, Suffolk Regt., only. Guides for "A" Company to be at junction of Railway and LILLE Road (I.14.c.7.8.) at 10.p.m.: guides for "C" Company to be at the junction of LILLE and WARRINGTON Roads at 10.p.m. All guides will be on the scale of 1 per platoon and Coy: Headquarters.

5. Platoons will move at 100 yards distance via WARRINGTON Road,— KRUISSTRAAT — SHRAPNEL CROSSING — VLAMERTINGHE.

carriage

6. TRANSPORT. One Limber per Company for of Lewis Guns, Ammunition, etc., will be 200 yards W. of GOLDFISH CHATEAU by 11.30.p.m. One Limber for Headquarters will be at I.8.6.10.80. (S. of MENINGATE) at 11.30.p.m. Application has been made for a truck on the Light Railway on returning ration train. O.C. Companies will send any Mess Kit which cannot be carried as far as the Limbers to B.H.Q. by the returning ration trolleys. One man per Company only need come down with this kit.

7. RATIONS for SUFFOLK Regiment will be pushed up to Companies' positions by "C" Company's pushing parties under the supervision of a Suffolk N.C.O., per Company.

8. ADVANCE PARTIES from the incoming unit will report during the day. All Trench Stores, work and defence schemes, and information concerning the Line will be carefully handed over. Store Lists to be forwarded to Orderly Room by 6.p.m. 7th inst.

8. The Quartermaster will arrange for all baggage from details to be taken to ORILLA CAMP by Light Railway in accordance with Brigade instructions in his possession, and also that meals are ready for the companies on arrival.

10. Arrangements for Baths and Pay on September 7th will be notified later.

11. 2/Lieut: H.RALPH will report to — H.L.I. at ORILLA CAMP, by 4.p.m. Sept: 6th and take over all stores, work and defence schemes.

12. Notification will be forwarded to Orderly Room immediately on arrival in billets.

13. The Guard in charge of Brigade S.A.A. Dump at SALLY PORT will not be relieved. This Guard will be rationed by the Front Line Battalion. Quartermaster will arrange for future reliefs. only 1 NCO

1 man will be left

Captain and Adjutant,
— Battalion Middlesex Regiment.

Battalion, Middlesex Regiment.

SECRET.　　Copy No: 16

Operation Order No: 21.　　10-9-15.

B.

1. The Battalion will relieve H.L.I. in SUPPORT on the night of Sept: 11/12th.

2. Relief will be carried out as follows:- as arranged direct between Company Commanders concerned:-

   Middlesex.　　　　　　　　H.L.I.
   "D" Company will relieve "A" Company, in I.14.c.
   "A" Company will relieve "C" Company, in CANAL BANK.
   "B" Company will relieve "B" Company, in HOOLOY HOUSE.
   "C" Company will relieve "D" Company, in H.12.a.

3. No guides will be provided.
   "C" Company will move via SLEEPER TRACK: remainder by main road.

4. One Limber per Company and one for Bn: H.Qrs: will bring up rations to companies during the afternoon and will then proceed up the line with them to carry Lewis Guns, etc. One water-cart will proceed up full to Battn: Headquarters, and remain there.

5. "D" Company will move off at 7.15.p.m. All movement will be by half platoons at 100 yards distance.

6. The usual advance parties will be sent up during the day to take over Trench Stores. These will be very carefully checked. Everything signed for must be accounted for at the end of the tour.

7. O.C. "C" Company will detail a Gas Guard of 1 N.C.O. and 5 men and 1 bugler (to be detailed from Headquarters) to proceed direct to Brigade H.Qrs: and mount at 7.45.p.m. The bugler will relieve the H.L.I. bugler. On the guard dismounting the bugler will remain there. One bugler (with bugle) will be attached to each Company H.Qrs: and Battn: H.Qrs: for the duration of the tour.

8. O.C. Companies will send in a nominal roll of all personnel of their company being left behind, by 10.a.m. tomorrow, stating why they are left behind.

9. All Blankets and Packs will be stacked near "A" Company's Office by 8.30.a.m. at a place to be detailed by the Regtl: Q.M.Sergt.

10. Relief will be wired by usual code word.

　　　　　　　　　　　(Sd) COLIN SMEE, Captain & Adjutant,
　　　　　　　　　　　　　Battalion Middlesex Regiment.

DISTRIBUTION:-

No: 1　"A" Coy:　　　　No: 10　Transport Officer.
　　2　"B" Coy:　　　　　　11　Medical Officer.
　　3　"C" Coy:　　　　　　12　- H.L.I.
　　4　"D" Coy:　　　　　　13　- Suffolks.
　　5　Second in Command.　14　R.S.M.
　　6　Adjutant.　　　　　　15　R.Q.M.S.
　　7　O i/c Signals.　　　16　War Diary.
　　8　Intelligence Offr:　17　File.
　　9　Quartermaster.

Secret. — Batn. The Middlesex Regt.
Operation Order No. 22.   Copy No. 10

Ref: Sheet 28 NW ¼ 1/10.000
         27 1/40.000

1. The Battalion will move from present positions tonight Sept 14/15th by train to School Camp 27/L 3 c 5 5.

2. The 1/1st Yorkshire Dragoons will relieve D Company under arrangements to be notified later.
The remaining Companies will not be relieved by anybody.

3. The Battalion will entrain at GODERICH SIDING I 1.c.1.8 at 10 pm as follows:-
There will be 2 trains of 13 trucks - 30 men per truck.
   1st Train   B & C Companies, and Headquarters less 2 Signallers & 1 Runner.
   2nd Train   A & D Companies & remainder of Hdqtrs.
The Brigade Intelligence Officer will be superintending the entraining of the Brigade, and Lieut E.C.P. Williams M.C. will superintend the entraining of the Battalion.

4. The Battalion will detrain at BLUE GRASS 27/F 28 c 19. and march to School Camp at 27/L 3 c 5 5.

5. Trench Stores etc in the case of 'D' Company will be handed over to 1/1st Yorkshire Dragoons and receipts obtained. Orders with regard to stores of remaining Companies will be issued later.

6. All baggage will be taken on the train, and must be carried from Companies positions to entraining point.

7. Completion of relief of D Company will be wired to this Office by code word MUD. Other companies will notify H.Q. Signals prior to disconnecting.

8. Transport is moving today under separate orders.

9. Advance parties have been arranged for.

10. Acknowledge by wire.

× distribution,
  overleaf.
14th Septr 1918.

Colin Lowe
Capt & Adjutant
Batn The Middx Regt.

Distribution

Copy No 1. to OC 'A' Company
2. - OC 'B' Company
3. - OC 'C' Company
4. - OC 'D' Company
5. - 2nd in Command
6. - Adjutant
7. - Medical Officer
8. - Signal Officer
9. - R.S.M.
10. - War Diary
11. - File

D

20th Battalion Middlesex Regiment.   Copy No. 12

SECRET.

Operation Order No. 25.   Sept. 20th, 1918

Reference Sheet 28.
1./40,000.

1. The Battalion will move today to relieve the 16th Battn. Manchester Regt., in DOMINION CAMP, G.23.b, and G.24.a.

2. The Battalion will move off at 7.p.m. in the following order, H.Q., 'A', 'B', Drums, 'C', 'D', Transport. Head of the Column to pass S.E. corner of the Camp at 7.0.p.m. proceeding in an Easterly direction. The usual intervals will be maintained throughout the march.

3. Baggage. Officers' valises and Mess kit will be dumped outside the Guard Room by 6.0.p.m. The Transport Officer will arrange to have a G.S.Wagon and the Mess Cart at the above place at 6.0.p.m. to collect same. Officers' servants will be responsible for loading this baggage.

4. Rations will be delivered in new Area.

5. All Trench maps, Air photos and Defence schemes will be taken over and receipted lists forwarded to Orderly Room as soon as possible.

6. Notification of arrival in billets will be sent to Battn. Orderly Room as soon as possible on completion.

7. It is to be impressed on all ranks that all movement, fires, smoke, lights etc., in the new area are to be reduced to a minimum. Any work done must not be allowed to show up as conspicuous alterations.

(Sd) COLIN SMEE,
Captain and Adjutant,
20th Battalion Middlesex Regiment.

DISTRIBUTION.

Copy No.1, to O.C. "A" Company.
     2.   - O.C. "B" Company.
     3.   - O.C. "C" Company.
     4.   - O.C. "D" Company.
     5.   - Second in Command.
     6.   - Adjutant.
     7.   - Signal Officer.
     8.   - Quartermaster.
     9.   - Transport Officer.
    10.   - Medical Officer.
    11.   - R.S.M.
    12.   - War Diary.
    13.   - File.

<u>Secret.</u> — Middlesex Regiment.

<u>Operation Order No. 24.</u> E.

Ref:- Sheet 28.

1/ Reliefs as follows will take place the night September 25th/26th.
10th H.L.I. will be relieved by 2 Coys 12th Suffolk Regt & 2 Coys 20th Middlesex Regt. under O.C. 12th Suffolk Regt. The 2 Coys of this Battalion will be 'D' Coy relieving Company of H.L.I. in RIGHT FRONT SECTOR and 'C' Coy relieving Company of H.L.I. in RESERVE. The remainder of the Battalion will remain in present positions.
The remaining 2 Coys of 12th Suffolk Regt will take over accommodation of vacated in DOMINION CAMP.

2/ Lorries conveying 12th Suffolk Regt forward will call at DOMINION CAMP at a time to be notified later, drop 2 Coys of 12th Suffolk Regt, pick up 'C' and 'D' Companies and convey the whole party to debussing point. M.28.d.9.8. 1 N.C.O. from each of 'C' & 'D' Coys will be on the road at the above time to lead 2 Coys 12th Suffolk Regt to their respective lines.

3/ Guides on the scale of 1 per Coy H.Q. and 1 per Platoon will be provided by 10th H.L.I. to be at debussing point at 7.30 p.m.

4/ Completion of relief of 'C' & 'D' Coys will be wired by code word to be obtained from O.C. 12th Suffolk Regt to 12th Suffolk Battalion Headquarters.

5. BAGGAGE

Officers' Valises, surplus mess kit, blankets in bundles of ten, greatcoats haversacks & entrenching tools (of men supplied with shovels) in labelled sandbags will be dumped under cover by Companies by 6 p.m. near Companies lines. These will be collected under arrangements to be made by the Transport Officer and taken to the Transport lines and stored under cover. A guard will be arranged later.

6. EXTRA EXPLOSIVES & R.E. STORES. will be drawn from Quartermaster's Stores tomorrow.- "D" Coy at 2 p.m.- C Coy at 3 p.m. approximately on the following scale, but the issue must be regulated by the amount of material in possession.

S.O.S. Rockets   - 3 per Company.
1" White V.P.A.   - 1 round per man
No 35 R.Grenades.   - 8 per rifle section
No 34 Egg bombs.   -   do
50 rds S.A.A. per man extra to 120 rounds carried.
24 No 27 smoke bombs per Coy.) To be kept
24 Phosphenous bombs per Coy.) in dry place.
Wire cutters   - 1 per section
Sandbags   - 3 per man
Picks   - every 10th man 1 pick
Shovels   - every other man 1 shovel

7. O's.C. Companies will notify R.Q.M.Sgt. by 10 p.m tomorrow the number of articles issued "per man" they require.
All tin discs and S.B.R. with white panel will be taken into the line.
Tommy cookers will be issued according to strengths of Companies, but should

not be used if any other method of cooking is available, as the supply is very limited and those at present in possession have to last until September 30th.

7. Arrangements for delivery of rations in the line are not yet known definitely, but probably they will be sent up by our own limbers. Rations for consumption 26th will be carried on the man.

8. Personnel earmarked for special duties, Courses, Reft Camp etc. will not be taken up the line but will be attached to 'A' Coy. from tomorrow at 6.p.m.
Nominal roll of such personnel to be rendered to Orderly Room by 12 noon tomorrow.

24-9-18

(Sd) Colin Snell
Captain & Adjutant.
20th Middlesex Regiment.

Distribution.

Copy No. 1 to O.C. 'A' Company
" " 2 " O.C. 'B' Company
" " 3 " O.C. 'C' Company
" " 4 " O.C. 'D' Company
" " 5 " Second in Command
" " 6 " Adjutant
" " 7 " Signal Officer
" " 8 " Transport Officer
" " 9 " Medical Officer
" " 10 " Intelligence Officer
" " 11 " R.Q.M. Sergt.
" " 12 " R.S.M.
" " 13 " 2 i/c
" " 14 " Orderly
" " 15 " File.

20th Battalion, Middlesex Regiment.   Copy No: 6.

SECRET.   Operation Order No: 25.   26-9-18.

1. The Battalion, less 2 Companies and Transport, and plus 2 Companies 12th Suffolk Regiment will move by march route from DOMINION CAMP to Forward Area, on night September 26th/27th.

2. GUIDES, as sent forward on the morning of September 26th will meet Companies at places to be notified later.

3. Dress will be ✛ Fighting Order for All Ranks. All surplus baggage: Mess Kit: Mens' Greatcoats, haversacks and entrenching tools (of men with shovels) in sandbags: blankets rolled in tens: will be dumped under cover near Companies Lines by 2.p.m. and will be taken to Transport Lines under arrangements to be made by the Transport Officer. The Quartermaster's Stores will move to the Transport Lines under arrangements to be made by the Transport Officer, to be clear of the camp by 5.30.p.m. Drums will be dumped at Q.M. Stores by 2.p.m.

4. The Transport Officer will arrange for one limber per Company and one for Headquarters to report to "A" and "B" Companies and H.Q. at 4.30.p.m. to carry forward Lewis Guns, Water Tins, etc. The Maltese Cart will report to the M.O. at 4.p.m. to remove surplus Medical Stores to the Transport Lines. The Mess Cart will report to H.Q. Mess at 4.p.m. to remove surplus Mess Kit and Orderly Room Stores.

5. Extra Explosives and R.E. Stores will be drawn from the Q.M. Stores by "A" Company at 2.p.m. and by "B" Company at 3.p.m.

6. "B" and "D" Companies, 12th Suffolk Regiment will stack all surplus kit under cover near their lines, and it will be removed by Transport Officer, 12th Suffolks.

7. Companies will march off in the following order:-
"A" Company, 20th Mdx: "B" Coy: 20th Mdx: "B" Coy: 12th Suffolk "D" Coy: 12th Suffolks, H.Q. 20th Middx:
Companies will move by Platoons at 100 yards intervals, at least. The Leading Platoon of "A" Company will leave Camp at 5.p.m.

8. Arrival in new positions will be reported to Battalion H.Q. by Runner - or if telephone communication is available by code word of Company Commander's name.

9. Intelligence men from "A" and "B" Company (including "C" and "D" Companies men) will report to the R.S.M. with full equipment by 4.45.p.m.

(sd)   COLIN SHEE, Captain and Adjutant,
        20th Middlesex Regiment.

TO:-
   2 i/c "A" Company,
   2 i/c "B" Company,
   O.C. "A" Company,
   O.C. "B" Company,
   2/Lieutenant C.H. MONTAGUE.

   Second in Command.   )
   O.C. "C" Company,   )
   O.C. "D" Company,   )   for
   Transport Officer.   )   information.
   Signal Officer.   )
   R.S.M.   )

1. The remainder of the Battalion is moving into the Forward Area on night September 26th/27th.

2. The Second in Command of "A" and "B" Companies and 2/Lieut: C.H. MONTAGUE for Headquarters, will proceed up to the Forward Area tonight in the Lorries conveying "C" and "D" Companies.
They will remain with the 12th Suffolk Regiment overnight, and will be informed of accommodation available by Brigade Intelligence Officer on morning of September 26th. They will reconnoitre the routes to this accommodation by day September 26th.

3. Guides as follows will report to Orderly Room at 7.a.m. tomorrow, Sept 26th:-
           1 per Platoon.   1 per Company H.Q. and 2 Bn: HQ rs., and
   in addition Corporal TRUSS with a bicycle.
These guides will proceed up to front line Battalion Headquarters, reporting to 2/Lieutenant C.H. MONTAGUE there at 11.a.m.
The Officers mentioned above will show their companies guides the routes by which the companies will move into accommodation; they will also select a spot for the guides to meet respective parties and this position they will send in to 2/Lieutenant C.H. MONTAGUE at 12th Suffolks Battalion Headquarters, written down.
2/Lieutenant C.H. MONTAGUE will forward all positions for meeting guides to Battalion H.Q. (DOMINION CAMP) by Corporal TRUSS.

4. DRESS. for Officers tonight will be Fighting Order.
   Dress for guides will be Fighting Order.

5. The Officers mentioned above will report at H.Q. Mess at 4.p.m. tonight.

                                                  Captain and Adjutant,
                                       20th Battalion, The Middlesex Regiment.

25-9-18.

SECRET.   OPERATION ORDER.   Copy No.
BY
Major W. W. Milne M.C.
Commanding - Bn. Middlesex Regiment

1. The Battalion will carry out an attack at a time and date to be notified later. The Battn. Suffolk Regt will be on our Left and the Battn. Wilts Regt will be on our Right.

2. OBJECTIVES.   1st Objective. Point on CANAL BANK O.4.a.15.85. along trench to N.E corner of TRIANGULAR WOOD. to S corner of TRIANGULAR WOOD, trench through O.3. central to point on RIGHT BN BOUNDARY. O.3.c.8.8.
   2nd Objective. Line running from point on CANAL BANK (O.5.a.30.15.) to WHITE CHATEAU along OAK SWITCH to Bn Right Boundary (O.4.c.50.40.)

3. BOUNDARIES. Battalion LEFT Boundary. South Bank of CANAL as far as TRIANGULAR BLUFF (O.5.a.5.2.)
   Battalion RIGHT Boundary I.32.c.60.80. - I.32.d.4.4. - O.3.c.85.85. - Road junction O.4.c.40.45
   Inter-Company Boundary. I.32 central - I.33.c.05.73. - (S of ARUNDEL) - I.33.c.5.3. - UPPER OOSTHOEK FARM. (Incl. to LEFT COY.) - to N E corner of TRIANGULAR WOOD (LOWER OOSTHOEK FM incl. to Right Coy.) - Straight line to WHITE CHATEAU.

4. DISPOSITIONS.   "A" Company - Right Front.
                   "B"   "   - Left Front.
                   "C"   "   - Right Support.
                   "D"   "   - Left Support.
                   Battn H.Q. - I.32.a.20.45.

2.

ASSEMBLY. All companies will be in position one hour before zero. Two front companies (A & B Companies) will be in position WEST of MIDDLESEX ROAD. 2 Platoons in 1st wave in "WORMS" 2 Platoons in 2nd wave in "WORMS" 50x in rear.

Two support companies ("C" & "D" Companies) will assemble in two waves of "WORMS" - 2 rear platoons on tape line, which will be laid from point on canal where light railway crosses it (I.32.b) to point on CONVENT LANE (I.32.c.5.9.). Flank sections will in all cases inter-lock with sections on their flanks.

O's C Companies will report to Battn. H.Q. immediately when in position.

6. BARRAGE. The Barrage will commence at zero - 5". There will be no preliminary bombardment. Barrage will lift at zero and move forward as fol:

1st	100 yards	-	3 mins.	=	zero + 3.
2nd	"	-	3 "	=	zero + 6.
3rd	"		3 "	=	" + 9.
4th	"		3 "		" + 12.
5th	"		6 "	=	" + 18.
6th	"		3 "	"	" + 21.
7th	"		3 "	"	" + 24.
8th	"		3 "	"	" + 27.
9th	"		3 "	"	" + 30.
10th	"		6 "	"	" + 36.
11th	"		3 "	"	" + 39.

First objective being reached, barrage will roll until zero + 96, at which time it will remain stationary for 4 mins. in front of first objective.

At zero + 100 barrage will continue to move forward at rate of 100 yds per 3 mins. up to zero + 124 when final objective will be reached.

At zero + 124 barrage will remain stationary for 5 mins. till zero + 129 and then cease.

3.

7. **ADVANCE.** All Companies will advance at zero hour. 'A' & 'B' Companies on reaching 1st objective will consolidate immediately. The time allowed for consolidation is from zero + 56 to zero + 96. ie. 163 minutes.

'C' & 'D' Companies will not pass through 'A' & 'B' Companies until zero + 100 when the barrage commences to move forward to second objective.

'A' & 'B' Companies cannot push out patrols on taking 1st objective owing to rolling barrage.

8. **REPORTS.** Capture of 1st objective will be reported to Bn. H.Q. (I.32.a.20.45) immediately by O's.C. 'A' & 'B' Coys and Bn. H.Q. will then move forward via CANAL BANK to I.33.a.2.45, to which place all further reports will be sent. Capture of final objective must be reported immediately.

9. **REINFORCEMENTS.** Any reinforcements sent up by the Support Companies will be reported to Bn H.Q. immediately by the O.C. Support Company concerned. Requests for reinforcements by 'A' & 'B' Companies will be sent to the support Company direct. Reinforcements must only be demanded in case of very urgent necessity.

10. **AEROPLANE CO-OPERATION.** (a) A CONTACT plane with streamer on the tail and a black flap on each lower plane, will fly along the front at zero + 120 minutes and after that at every successive hour until further orders. All tin discs and white panels on S.B.R. of LEADING TROOPS will be shewn on demand.
(b) A COUNTER ATTACK Aeroplane will patrol the front from zero + 40 minutes onwards and will signal the development of an enemy counter-attack by firing a RED parachute flare.

11. **MISCELLANEOUS.** Prisoners will be sent to Bn. H.Q. under lowest escort possible.

R.A.P. will be established at H.30.Central.
No dugouts will be entered until reported free from mines by Tunnellers who will mark all dugouts "EXAMINED" or "DANGEROUS".
General compass bearing of attack is 140° magnetic from MIDDLESEX ROAD.

Colin Surrey
Capt & Adjutant Middlesex R.

"A" Form
MESSAGES AND SIGNALS.

Army Form C. 2121
(in pads of 100).

No. of Message............

Prefix......Code......m.	Words	Charge	This message is on a/c of:	Recd. at......m.
Office of Origin and Service Instructions.				Date......
3/4pm	Sent At ......m.		............Service	From......
	To......			By......
	By......	(Signature of "Franking Officer")		

TO: ~~Gen~~ MEVE

| Sender's Number | Day of Month | In reply to Number | AAA |
| S 11 | 28 | | |

Please convey heartiest congratulations of all got and myself ranks you on all success brilliant

2.3pm
28th

From: Brigadier Vale
Place:
Time:

The above may be forwarded as now corrected. (Z)

.... Censor. Signature of Addressor or person authorised to telegraph in his name.

* This line should be erased if not required.

O.C. A Coy 20th Middx
" B " "
" C " "
" D " "
" B " H.L.I.

The line will be reorganised as follows.

"D" Coy Middx in depth on original front.

"C" Coy Middx in depth on original front.

O.C. "C" Coy must get in touch with builts on right about "RUINED FARM" and get them to join up at O.4.c.4.4.

"B" Coy Middx will organise in depth on lines O.4.a.3.3 and O.4.a.6.6. and O.3.b.5.3 to O.3.b.95.60.

"A" Coy Middx will organise in depth on lines O.3.d.69.15 to O.3.b.95.15. and thence "A" brook to TRIANGULAR WOOD

O.C. "A" Coy will get in touch with builts support on right.

If "C" Coy can keep touch with WILTS on right. The platoon from H.Z.I. will consolidate LOWER DOSTHOEK FARM. If this is not possible this H.Z.I. platoon will fill gap between C Coy & WILTS

H.Z.I platoon now with A Coy will consolidate UPPER GOSTHOEK FARM

C.H.Q. remaining & 2 platoons of B Coy H.Z. will remain in present position.

Front line patrols will be put out not more than 300 yards during the night

These H.Q. will be notified immediately these alterations have been completed.

W. L. Mitchel
Major
Commdg 5o the middlesex Regt

4.30 pm
28.9.18

MESSAGE AND SIGNALS.

TO: A B C & D Companies
b/15 Suffolk (from ?) L

Sender's Number.	Day of Month.	In reply to Number.	A A A
*CS 9	29		
at	5.30am	WILTS	~~left~~ on
your ~~will~~	night	&	34th
Division	on	their	right
will	move	Eastward	aaa
ourselves	&	Suffolks	will
move	forward	at	the
same	time	keeping	touch
aaa	C	Company	must
gain	touch	with	WILTS
by	that	hour	aaa
Scouts	&	patrols	must
go	ahead	of	platoons
and	flanks	must	be
carefully	kept	in	touch
aaa	Companies	will	make
good	well	organised	pieces
of	trench	and	report

From
Place
Time

"A" Form.
MESSAGES AND SIGNALS.

Situation	aaa
frequently on	situation	aaa
our left	must	hug
the canal	&	our
right conform	to	the
WILTS aaa	A	Company
will conform	with	movements
in front	but	B
Company will	not	move
until further	orders	

From
Place Aubert
Time 5.0am

OC A Coy 20th Mid'x
OC B " "
OC D Coy HLI
OC 12th H.L.I. R.S.
OC 16th H.L.I.

1.) The Right front Company (C Coy) will push forward to occupy the ridge from THE STABLES to O.5.c.2.
The left front Coy will push forward and occupy J.X.E.O.5.c.2.2 to O.5 central.
Right Support Company will advance to MAIN CHATEAU line.
Left Support will remain in present position.
B Coy HLI will remain in present position.

2.) When this line THE STABLES to O5 central is made good the Right Company will pivot on the STABLES & advance its left to S.E. C.11.a.10.95.
The left Company will advance

2 (Continued)
O.N.a.10.95 on the right
and O.5.d.2.2.
A Coy from WHITE CHATEAU
will keep in touch with "D"
and keeping left on Canal
will advance to OBLIQUE
TRENCH

3. "D" Coy will again move
forward keeping right on
O.11.a.10.80. and swinging
left round to O.11.b.25.50.
"A" Coy keeping touch with
left of "D" will advance & get
touch with 41st Div in
~~HOLLEBEKE.~~ LOCK 5.
The line will then run from the
STABLES ——— LOCK 5.
The platoon of "B" Coy H.L.I.
will remain in same position
and act as defensive flank

W W Nulne
Major
Comdg Middlesex Rgt

29-9-18
9.0 am

WAR DIARY.

20th Bn MIDDLESEX REGT.

October 1918.

WAR DIARY
INTELLIGENCE SUMMARY.

Army Form C. 2118.

OCTOBER 1915

Place	Date	Hour	Summary of Events and Information	Remarks and references to Appendices
SMYTHE'S FARM	1/10/15		Mobilization Stores checked. Deficiencies in small kit ascertained. Cleaning and improvement of shelters carried on. Orders received for move N.E. of YPRES.	
	2nd	6.15am	Battalion moved by march route via VRUISSTRAAT and	
POTIJZE		8.45	YPRES to field near POTIJZE where tents were pitched and huts erected. Lorries to convey sandbags, corrugated greatcoats and overcoats, and blankets did not report at right place. Lorries sent for but arrived very late in the afternoon — one lorry broke not — down until next morning. Orders received for working parties 3rd inst.	
	3rd	4am	A.& B. Coys and part of B. & H. & D. paraded at 4 a.m. and proceeded to CLAPHAM JUNCT. near HOOGE for the purpose of filling in craters. This party was relieved by remainder of Bn. at crater at 7.30 p.m. These Companies continued until 7.30 when they returned to Camp.	
	4th		Working parties same as yesterday. Scene of operations now between INVERNESS COPSE and GHELUVELT. Buses were arranged	

WAR DIARY
or
INTELLIGENCE SUMMARY.
(Erase heading not required.)

Army Form C. 2118.

OCTOBER 1918

Place	Date	Hour	Summary of Events and Information	Remarks and references to Appendices
POTIJZE	4th		for O/O Coy hut on arrival at huts, he Coy found them not working. A&B Coys halted during afternoon + other and fast of old Bay halted during evening, clean lines being drawn for the remainder.	
	5th		Remainder of A&B Coys bathed. Working parties as usual. Remainder in a tarpaulin erected in camp.	
		6.45	Details and a draft of 50, together with the Band, sent from the 21st Bn MIDDLESEX Regt. arrived. Four of the draft were found to have been admitted to hospital. The draft was posted to Coys/Companies according to relative strengths in order to make them equal.	
	6th		The draft and casuals bathed from 0800 – 1630 and were inspected by the M.O. The Brigadier General visited the Battalion in order to inspect the draft.	
	7th		Working parties as usual	
	8th		All Companies proceeded on working parties in morning	

WAR DIARY
or
INTELLIGENCE SUMMARY

(Erase heading not required.)

Army Form C. 2118.

OCTOBER 1918.

Place	Date	Hour	Summary of Events and Information	Remarks and references to Appendices
POTIJZE	Oct 8th		Two companies reported for work at 7 a.m. and the others at 8 a.m. Work today ended at 3 p.m. and companies returned to camp by 4.15 p.m.	
	9th		Work same as usual	
	10th		" " " "	
	11th		On 11th the Commanding officer, Major W.O. Milne M.C. proceeded on leave and Major Hush assumed command of the battalion. Warning orders for a move to the WULVERGHEM area were received.	
WULVERGHEM	12th		Reveille at 4.30 a.m. Tents were struck and loaded on lorries, as were blankets and sandbags containing men's spare kit. These lorries proceeded to the camp to be erected in the new area. The Battalion entrained at HELLFIRE CORNER and proceeded via YPRES, HAZEBROUCK to WULVERGHEM where the Battalion detrained and marched to camp. Tents were pitched — with intervals of about 25 yds between tents.	
	13th		The day was devoted to cleaning up and improving camp.	

WAR DIARY
INTELLIGENCE SUMMARY
(Erase heading not required.)

Army Form C. 2118.

Place	Date	Hour	Summary of Events and Information	Remarks and references to Appendices
WULVERGHEM	13th		An R.E. Service was held in camp occupied by 13th Suffolk Regt.	
		11.30pm	The enemy commenced shelling, two shells pitched in the camp in B Company's lines. One NCO was wounded and one officer.	
	14th		The shelling continued at intervals for about 1½ hours, the great majority of the shells going over the camp and falling near that occupied by the 12th Suffolk Regt.	
		4 am	Shelling recommenced this time by H.V. Gun and ordinary gun. Shells fell all about the camp. The line held by the 13th Bn was reconnoitred by the Commanding Officer and Company Commanders. 2nd in Command of Companies reconnoitred line to be taken up as required according to defence scheme.	
WERWICQ	15th		The Battalion moved by stages to WERWICQ where it relieved the 7th Bn Royal Irish Regt, which was supposed to be holding the front line, but earlier in the day the Suffolk Battalion had passed through and crossed the LYS, so the Battalion	

WAR DIARY
INTELLIGENCE SUMMARY.
(Erase heading not required.)

Army Form C. 2118.

OCTOBER 1918.

Place	Date	Hour	Summary of Events and Information	Remarks and references to Appendices
WERVICQ.	15th		was in support, O.T.C. companies in the front line and B+D in support, half of the men were accommodated in pillboxes and inside quite comfortable.	
	16th		Line was quiet except for occasional shelling of bridges over-tys near the church in WERVICQ.	
	17th		Received warning orders to move forward across Lys in support of two front line battalions which had occupied RONCQ. Battalion moved during afternoon and evening, some difficulty being experienced in crossing the Lys owing to bridges being so narrow and unstable. Bn H.Qrs were established at KIT HOUSE.	A.
RONCQ.	18th		Battalion advanced through 13th Suffolk Regt to line E. of MOUSCRON, B again RONCQ at 10 a.m. The Commanding officer and advanced Bn H.Qrs passed through TOURCOING receiving a great many cheers of the joy of the inhabitants on being released from enemy rule.	B.
TOURCOING				
MOUSCRON.			The Battalion took up the line as stated in orders and	

WAR DIARY
or
INTELLIGENCE SUMMARY

Army Form C. 2118.

OCTOBER 1918.

Place	Date	Hour	Summary of Events and Information	Remarks and references to Appendices
MOUSCRON	18th/19th		met opposition in the later stages of the operation. Patrols were held all night, opposition slackening in the early hours of the morning. One prisoner was taken, in civilian clothes, who had apparently been living with civilians for some weeks.	
	19th		Line established on final objective at about 6.0 a.m. Orders to move & occupy line E of PETIT VOISINAGE & MARCENSE. No opposition met with & line easily established, in some cases beyond S[?]richie which was difficult to pick up.	C.
		2.0 pm	GOC Division gave verbal orders to move forward, as enemy was reported found, to a line between CROIX ROUGE & DOTTIGNIES. Patrol under 2/L G.F. PLEDGER had previously entered DOTTIGNIES & only seen a few isolated Huns one of whom he shot. Line established about 6.0 pm though returned with Suffolks on the right who had moved some 2 hours previously & London Scottish (2/14 London Rgt. 30th Divn.) on the left. A fortnight flash of rain rations lost.	
	19/20th		Orders received for move on 20th inst 1st & 2 Objectives (both taken) 1st Objective a line about	

WAR DIARY
or
INTELLIGENCE SUMMARY.
(Erase heading not required.)

Army Form C. 2118.

October 1918

Place	Date	Hour	Summary of Events and Information	Remarks and references to Appendices
MOUSCRON	10/20		500x W of COYGHEM – WARCOING Road as Objective the West Bank of the River l'ESCAUT (or SCHELD).	
		2045	Move commenced at 8.0 a.m. Some slight opposition offered passing through DOTTIGNIES but mainly on left flank from COYGHEM though ground of that place – very heavy shelling of DOTIGNIES after our troops had passed it. First Objective reached about 10.0 a.m. of which with Pak flaks. Resistance practically nil, the enemy not waiting to use his MGs to any particular effect. Artillery (118 Bde & Pak Bde 51st Batln) opened fire on batteries reported E of Coyghem and was shelled in reply with great accuracy very shortly after opening fire – also Bn Headquarters. A spy was later brought at Bn Headquarters who chosen originally owing to shelling	D.
		11.00	of telephone nearby by another unit. An Headquarters moved forwards but could not take up position at that chosen originally owing to shelling – reports consequently delayed a good deal.	
		12.00	Bn Headquarters moved up to CHERQUANT FARM, but it was not possible to let all Companies know about this move consequently reports still further delayed. Final Objective reached about 5.0 p.m. by right Company	

WAR DIARY
INTELLIGENCE SUMMARY

October 1918

Place	Date	Hour	Summary of Events and Information	Remarks and references to Appendices
DOTIGNIES / ESPIERRES	20th		but left Company had to swing right round & pass through ESPIERRES as the only means of crossing the R. GRAND ESPIERRES. Whole Machine taken & posts established at about 5.0pm. Left was at junction of L'ENFER - HELCHIN - ESPIERRES Roads & Right at ESPIERRES Canal Bridge. In touch with 12th Suffolks on the Right & 5th Canal in front in touch with London Scottish on left, who had however belongs E. of OOGHEM - defensive flank therefore formed by swinging back left flank & pushing up two platoons of Support Company on Grand Espierres River & reinforcing flank with M.G. Section. London Scottish came up at about 7.0pm however & flank resumed notional positions. Final dispositions being B Company on left & D Company on the right, each with 2 platoons in forward posts & 2 platoons W. of HELCHIN-ESPIERRES Road. A Company in Support at Crucifix Cross Roads west of ESPIERRES & C Company in Reserve at BOIS JACQUET. A distressing - (roran) positions shelled. Sniped. Machine Gunned & Trench Mortared. Our positions Gas shelled. This slackened off towards midnight &	

WAR DIARY
INTELLIGENCE SUMMARY

Army Form C. 2118.

October 1918

Place	Date	Hour	Summary of Events and Information	Remarks and references to Appendices
BOTTIGNIES / ESPIERRES.	20th cont		Enemy contented himself with harassing fire on villages & farm houses. Civilians of ESPIERRES greatly assisted our troops in taking village by helping to build the bridge.	
	20/21st		Patrols pushed out, but could not cross l'ESCAUT - ground all round river & canal very marshy. T.B. of river all flooded. Rations got up. A prisoners drove into our left Company in a car having lost their way - belonged to administration troops - doubtful if they meant to lose their way - civilians from different places coming in. - S.A.A got up & wounded brought down. Total casualties 20 killed 70 wounded.	
	21st		Enemy continued harassing fire on horses etc but did not shell positions much, but sniping & M.Gs very active on fire positions & any movement in spite of fact that position taught be out of views. This leads to spys in ESPIERRES & 1 Belgian Carrier pigeon shot on a horse top, but no time to search lofts, or houses. More civilians - 13 men & 2 women - from HELCHIN - making a total of 24 civilians sent down. Arrangements for relief by - Manchesters.	

WAR DIARY
INTELLIGENCE SUMMARY.
(Erase heading not required.)

Army Form C. 2118.

October 1918

Place	Date	Hour	Summary of Events and Information	Remarks and references to Appendices
Frasnes lez Buissenal	21st		arrangements very hastily made only commenced at 6 p.m. Complete by about 11:30 p.m. Battalion moved back to western edge of DOTIGNIES	
DOTIGNIES	22nd		Resting. Billets good & men made much of by civilians.	
	23rd		Resting in the morning. Moved back to HUINGNE in the afternoon.	E.
HUINGNE	24th		Cleaning up & refitting. Baths & pay. Final arrival of all late stragglers & numerous places since commencement of advance.	
	25th		Training commenced. One section of T.M. Battery joined Battalion	F.
	26th		Training continued. Draft of 1 Off. and 49 O.Rs joined Bn. 10 employed with DADOS.	
	27th		Cleaning up Church Parades at the Convent. Inspection of aircraft	
	28th		Training in the use of advance guards.	G.
	29th		Outpost scheme practised. The B.G.C. visited companies while carrying out these schemes.	
	30th		Training as usual. Lecture by D.Q.O. to all Officers.	
	31st		Training as usual. 3 gas shells in the vicinity 5H.5 village about 7.0 a.m.	
		15.15	G.O.C. lectures to all Officers NCOs on Open warfare in the afternoon.	
		19.00	Information received that TURKEY capitulated at 12 noon.	

J.J. Newnham Major
Cmdg 20th Middlesex Regt.

Sheet. 28.SE.

Move Orders No 1.
O.O. No. 28.   **A**

SECRET.

I. The Enemy are believed to have evacuated LILLE TOURCOING and ROUBAIX.

II. 12th Suffolks & 10th H.L.I are taking up a line from RONCQ to x.25 central. inclusive. (Left Boundary being grid line x.7 central to x.8 central)

III. The Battalion will take up positions in Support in the LINSELLES SWITCH as follows:—

C Company on the right from road running from CRUST CROSS (W.10.c.) to BANDY FARM (W.16.b) as approx. Right Boundary; to road running through W.10.b. to RICHE VILLAGE & W.11 central as left boundary. on the left,

A Company from C Company left boundary to road running through W.5. immediately West of GRAND WOOD.

D Company in right support in area around KIN HOUSE & W.10.a.

B Company in left support in area between CEMETERY in W.4.b & GRAND CHÊNE FARM. in W.4.d.

Bn HQ will probably be at KITH HOUSE W.3.b. 95. 05.

IV. Companies will move as soon as possible after receipt of these orders as follows:—

C & D Companies via Bridge at P.36.a.2.7. by best available route to PAUL BNCQ thence to positions.

A & B Companies via Bridge at Q.27.b.0.5.

Companies will move in small columns, prepared to provide their own protection if necessary, but will in no way interfere with the movement of troops of the Suffolks or 11th I. who are both in positions in front.

O's C Companies will notify Bn HQ over the 'phone immediately prior to moving off, & will report as soon as possible when in new positions

V. The 42 Brigade are moving to LINSELLES-LE BLATON area. OC C Company will obtain touch with them as soon as possible after arrival in position
OC A Company will endeavour to obtain connection with Troops of 30th Division on the left.

VI. The 46th Bde RFA will cover the Brigade.

VII. Rations. Guides & usual ration parties from B & D ~~1st~~ Companies will report at ~~Bn HQ~~ KITH HOUSE at ~~9pm~~ 21.00 hrs. Water this will be taken forward.

VIII Acknowledge by wire

17/10/18

Col Sure
Capt Adjt
20th Middlesex

Move Orders No 2   B

Refshas
9799.

1. The enemy is reported to be retiring to the E & SE towards TOURNAI. He will probably attempt to delay us by holding railway running NNW & SW at MOUSCRON

2. #3rd Brigade will move forward with 2oh Middlesex on right & on the left 10th H.L.I and will take up line running from A5 central through S'30 central S'24 central & S17 central and thence along Rly to Cross line just S of PETIT CORNIT

3. Left Battalion boundary will be the line X 13 d 40 45 on RONCR - to BLANC FOUR Rd to S'24 a. Right Battalion boundary will be approximately from X'75 central to A5 central.

4. Companies will advance from present positions in

2/

sufficient time to cross RONCQ-
BLANC FOUR Road at 10.00.
'A' Company on left 'C' on
right. 'B' Coy left support
'D' on right Support.
Inter Company boundary
will be x 19 d 7.5. — 5.30 Central
Companies will move in
depth covered by small
columns in single file
preceded by Scouts.
Company Commanders will
have the line of advance
reconnoitred by immediately
despatching patrols to
pass the suffocks on receipt
of these orders.
They will question
inhabitants as to whether
the advance would be
best across fields or
whether it is best to keep
to the road. also as to
any possible mines or
booby traps (list of those
reported attached)

5/ all bridges over the Canal
round TOURCOING are reported
destroyed.

3

6. Support Companies will follow up front Companies 300x in rear keeping touch & will take up positions 200x in rear of objective.

7. Suffolks become support Battalion and move to line running NE & through RONQUONS TOUT.
Should Divisions on left & right not move, 43rd Bde will move independently covering own flanks.

8. One section A Battery 116 Bde R.F.A. will be attached to Right Battalion.

9. Mounted troops are moving across RONCQ - BLANC FOUR Road at 0900 hours. Report being sent back by them to Bdehqrs in jones which will be forwarded to B HQ as soon as possible.

10. Battn Hdqrs will be at x20a.92 at 1000 hours & will move to Cross Roads Sq central at about 1100 hours.

Colin Snell
Capt & Adjt

Move Orders
No. 3

C/

1. The 43rd Bde will push forward today Oct 19th to occupy the line from B.13.c.00.00 to B.7.c.10.00 – T.25.d.20.80 to T.19.d.60.60 – PETIT VOISINAGE inclusive.
   The 12th Suffolk Regt will be on the Right and 20th Middlesex on the Left.

2. Inter Battalion Boundary being B.1.d.10.25. The 12th Suffolk Regt will move from present positions (S.W.) at 09.00 hours and when they reach right flank B & D Companies will move forward in conjunction with them.

3. Inter Company Boundary will be approx the grid line through S.30 central and T.25 central inclusive to D Coy.
   B & D Coys will be in positions immediately in rear of B & C Coys respectively by not later than 09.30 hours ready to move forward immediately the Suffolks come up on the Right Flank. OC D Coy must arrange with OC B Coy

3 cont'd

2.

so that the information is passed to 'B' Coy by the quickest possible method.

4. OC 'A' Coy will move one platoon North of the LUINGNE - PETIT-VOISINAGE Road in support of B Coy's left flank.

5. C Coy will be in support & will move by platoons in artillery formation along the inter-company boundary with 3 platoons North of this line.

6. 'A' Coy (less 1 platoon mentioned above) will be in reserve as soon as 'B' Coy have passed through LUINGNE but until such time will be in immediate support to this Coy.

On coming into Reserve A Coy will move forward on the grid line between S.24 and S.30. & T.19 and T.25. When the objective is reached.

C Coy will take up position from approximately T.25.c.55.90 to B.1.a.2.8. disposed in depth and 'A' Coy will take up a position in depth along an approximate cont/ 3.

line from T.25.a.05.40. to
T.19.c.30.50 with 3 platoons.
'A' Coy 4th Platoon will form
a defensive flank North of road
through T.19. Central conforming
to 'B' Companies left flank, which
should cover the North side of
road junction T.19.b.4.1.

VIII Bn H.Q will be established at
road junction S.29.d.2.7. at
09.15 hours and will move to
WINDMILL S.30.b.5.0. at 11.00 hrs

IX Objective should be reached by
14.00 hrs at latest.

X The 10th H.L.I will not move until
all the objectives which should
have been taken on 18th instant
have been captured. They will
then move into support in A.5.
c + d area.

19-10-18.   (sd) Colin Smee
                 Captain & adjt.
                 20th Middlesex Regt

Move Orders No 4

Ref Sheets 29 & 36 1/40000.   D

1. The Battalion will be prepared to move forward again tomorrow Dec 20th at ~~0500 hours~~ in conjunction with the 17th Suffolks on the right and take up the following line T30 b 10.60 – T30 b 10.00 – B6 b 10.00 – B6 d 10.00 – Bty Central.

2. Boundaries. Left Boundary will be the River line.
Right Boundary will be line from QUEVAUCAMP to Bty Central crossing Railway at B11 a 7.7. Inter Coy Boundary will be from the V of La CROIX ROUGE through T29 c 0.0 – B5 b 1.8 – B6 a 0.6 – B6 b 2.1 (Road through B5 b & B6 a inclusive to Right Company)

3. Dispositions. B & D Companies will continue the advance in the usual formations of worms. A' Company will be in support "move 300x" in rear of leading Companies approx along inter-coy boundary with

2

one platoon North & 2 platoons South of this Boundary. The Company will pass DOTTIGNIES with 1 platoon to the North & 2 platoons to the SOUTH. The remaining platoon pushing through the town.
'C' Coy will be in reserve & will follow 300x in rear of Support Company passing through DOTTIGNIES in the same manner.

4. Both B & D Companies will report to BHQ when crossing line running from Railway crossing at B11 b.1580 along the street through B5 c & a and T29 c & d to left boundary.

5. BHQ will move first to buildings at T28 c 1030 to which place reports will be sent as called for in para 4 and also reports on reaching final objective. Further movement of BHQ will then be notified.

6. O.C. Coys will arrange for their respective M.G. Sections

3

to move with their Companies.
7. On arrival at final objective
 A Coy will take up position
 in support of B Coy & C Coy
 in support of D Coy
8. It is not known if Division
 on left is moving or not
 If not O.C. "A" Coy will
 arrange to cover B Coy's
 left flank.

for Capt & Adjt
9th Middlesex Regt

19.10.18.

Addendum to Move Orders No 4

1. There will be a 2nd objective today, Oct 20th which will be the West Bank of the River ESCAUT. On reaching this objective a line will be taken up parrallel to the River (along the HELCHIN – ESPIERRES Road) with posts pushed well forward to cover the river approaches.

2. Boundaries. N. Brigade boundary (Left Bn. Boundary) has been altered to be as follows:–
   From C.6.6. to C.4.a.3.0.
   Inter Battn Boundary is the line from B.10.a.4.6. B.12.c.5.3. to W Bank of Canal and thence along Canal Bank.
   Inter Company boundary will be line from B.4.a.7.6. to C.4.b.2.9.
   1st objective remains the same within these limits.
   B & D Coys will continue the advance from the 1st objective to the second objective. On reaching the first objective the Battn will halt for 15 minutes

2.

to adjust the line, and ensuring in touch on the <u>inner flanks</u> of the 2 Front Companies.

They will not proceed forward of this line until touch with one another is obtained in any case.

The outer flanks must be protected by Support Company if touch has been lost with units on the flank.

O.C. "B" "D" Coys will report to Bn.H.Q. when on the first objective. Bn H.Q. will be situated at building immediately N. of Rue de la BELLE-VUE (B.4. a. 9. 8) for this report.

At the end of 15 minutes halt the Battalion will move forward to line of main road from H.25.a. to C.7.c. and will again halt on this line for 15 minutes, at the end of which time the advance will continue normally to the final objective.

4) Ref para 5 of Move orders No 3. The report centre for these

reports will be B.3 C, S.2
(Batt. C + D Coys Headquarters)

5. OC's Support & Reserve Coys will keep Bn HQ informed continuously of their approx C.H.Q. positions and where orders are to be sent (approximately)

6. It is believed that the enemy will hold the west bank of the River L'ESCAUT with MGs and that the river is wired on both banks. All wire cutters available will be taken.

7. Report on Rivers attached.

8. Further locations of Companies will be notified later.

20/10/17

(Sd) Colin Lyall
Capt & Adjutant

LESPIERRES RIVER

Width in metres
at water level — 16.00 M
Width at bed level — 10.00 M
Depth — 2.00 M
Width of tow path — 4.00 M

L'ESCAUT RIVER

Very marshy & liable to inundations, numerous irrigation ditches
depth not known
width not known

"A" Form
MESSAGES AND SIGNALS.

Army Form C. 2121
(in pads of 100).

No. of Message............

Prefix........Code........m.	Words	Charge	This message is on a/c of	Recd. at ......m..
Office of Origin and Service Instructions.				
....	Sent		..................Service	Date............
....	At........m.			From............
....	To............			
....	By............		(Signature of "Franking Officer")	By............

TO {

Sender's Number	Day of Month	In reply to Number	**A A A**

From
Place
Time

The above may be forwarded as now corrected.   **(Z)**

....
Censor.   Signature of Addressor or person authorised to telegraph in his name

* This line should be erased if not required.

(7700.) Wt. W192/M1647 110,000 Pads 5/17 C & R. Ltd. (E. 1187.)

20th Battn: Middlesex Regt.

SECRET.   Operation Order No: 30.   22-10-18.

1. The Battalion will move to LUINGNE tomorrow, Oct: 23rd, 1918.

2. Order of march will be - B.H.Q., "B","C","D","A",Transport.
   Head of the column will pass B.H.Q. at 1430 hours.

3. Companies will move by platoons at 100 yards intervals.
   Strict march discipline will be maintained.

4. BAGGAGE. Officers' valises will be stacked as follows at 1300 hours.
   "A","B" & "D" Coys at the X. Roads; "C" & H.Q. at Bn: Headqrs:
   The Mess Cart will collect Mess Kit commencing at 1330 with "B" Coy.
   The Maltese Cart will report to the Medical Officer at 1330 hours.
   Lewis Gun Limbers will be loaded under order of the L.G.Officer.

5. Teas will be served on arrival.
   Headquarter cooking utensils will be carried on the cookers.

6. Advance parties as already detailed.

                    (sd) COLIN SMEE, Captain and Adjutant,
                         20th Bn: Middlesex Regiment.

DISTRIBUTION:-
  O.C. "A" Company,   Lewis Gun Officer
     "B" Company,   Medical Officer.
     "C" Company,   Signals.
     "D" Company,   Regtl: Sergt: Major,
  Quartermaster,   War Diary.
  Transport Officer.   File.

20th Battalion Middlesex Regiment.

TRAINING PROGRAMME - Oct. 25th/26th.

F.

Date.	Hours.	Subject.
OCTOBER 25TH 1918.	0830/0900 hrs. 0900/0945 " 0945/1115 " 1130/1215 " 1215/1230 "	Company Commanders' Inspection. Close Order Drill. Advanced Guards. Physical Training. Gas.
		SPECIALIST CLASSES.
	0915 hrs.	Lewis Gun Class, under Bn. L.G.Officer. (8 men per Company) Signallers under Signalling Officer (4 Signallers per Coy. & H.Q.Signallers) Snipers under Bn. Sniping Officer. (4 Snipers per Coy. and H.Q.Snipers)
	1000 hrs.	Stretcher Bearers. 4 Stretcher Bearers per Company under Medical Officer.)
OCTOBER 26TH 1918.	0830/0900 hrs. 0900/0945 " 0945/1115 " 1130/1215 " 1215/1230 "	Company Commanders' Inspection. Bayonet Fighting. Out-posts. Close Order Drill. Gas.
		SPECIALIST CLASSES.
	0915 hours.	Lewis Gun Class.) under Signallers.) Specialist Snipers.) Officers.
	1000 hours.	Stretcher Bearers under Medical Officer.

NOTE. Following points to be brought out during Training.

    Smart turnout on first parade.
    Drill parades to be commanded by Officers, not N.C.Os.
    ADVANCED GUARDS. Keeping touch. Columns moving across open country. Guarding flanks and covering gaps.
    OUTPOSTS. Advanced groups posted with a view to giving as much rest as possible to men not on duty. Posting of sentries at night guarding lines of approach rather than open country. Communications.
    P.T. & B.F.Parades. Men to be kept at work for full ¾ hour, otherwise hours of parade will have to be increased.

24-10-1918.

                                              Captain and Adjutant,
                20th Battalion Middlesex Regiment.

20TH BATTALION MIDDLESEX REGIMENT.

Training Programme for week October 28th – November 2nd 1918.

DATE.	HOURS.	SUBJECT.
MONDAY OCTOBER 28TH.	0830 – 0900 0900 – 0930 0930 – 1000 1000 – 1045 1045 – 1100 1100 – 1230 1415 – 1445	Company Commanders' Inspection. Physical Training. Bayonet Fighting. Close Order Drill. Gas. Advance Guards. Map Reading under Platoon Commanders for N.C.Os and selected Privates.
	Specialist Classes as on 25th and 26th Oct. in addition.	
	1415 – 1515	Organised Games.
TUESDAY OCTOBER 29TH.	0830 – 0900 0900 – 0930 0930 – 1000 1000 – 1045 1045 – 1100 1100 – 1230 1415 – 1445	Company Commanders' Inspection. Physical Training. Bayonet Fighting. Close Order Drill Gas. Outposts. Message writing under Platoon Commanders for N.C.Os and selected Privates.
	Specialist Classes to continue.	
	1415 – 1515	Organised Games.
WEDNESDAY OCTOBER 30TH.	0830 – 0900 0900 – 0930 0930 – 1000 1000 – 1045 1045 – 1100 1100 – 1230 1415 – 1445	Company Commanders' Inspection. Physical Training. Bayonet Fighting. Close Order Drill. Gas. Attack on Strong points by Platoons. Map reading as on previous days.
	Specialist Classes to continue	
THURSDAY OCTOBER 31ST.	0830 – 1045 1045 – 1230 1415 – 1445 1415 – 1515	As on previous days Attack Practice by Companies. Message writing as before. Organised Games.
	Specialist Classes to continue.	
FRIDAY NOVEMBER 1ST.	0830 – 1045 1045 – 1230 1415 – 1445	As on previous days. Companies at disposal of Company Commanders for Tactical Scheme. Games.
SATURDAY NOVEMBER 2ND.	0830 – 0900 0900 – 1030 1045 – 1230	Company Commanders Inspection. Battalion Parade. Companies Tactical Schemes.

27/10/1918.

Captain and Adjutant
for Major,
Commanding 20th Battalion Middlesex Regiment.

War Diary

20th Middlesex Regt

November 1918

WAR DIARY

20th Bn MIDDLESEX REGT
NOVEMBER 1918

WAR DIARY
or
INTELLIGENCE SUMMARY.
(Erase heading not required.)

Army Form C. 2118.

NOVEMBER 1918

Place	Date	Hour	Summary of Events and Information	Remarks and references to Appendices
November LUINGNE	1st		The Battalion paraded at 9 a.m. when it was inspected by the Commanding Officer - Major C.S. Muck. Training carried out later than training programme. A warning order for a move was received during the day. Answers received of the award of the Military Medal to five men for bravery during active operations on 20/21 Oct.	
	2nd		Training as per training programme. Orders issued for a move on the 3rd.	A1
PETIT AUDENARDE	3rd		The Battalion moved at 10.00 hrs. to PETIT AUDENARDE and the billets in new area were occupied by 13.00 hrs and found to be good generally. The lorry supplied for carrying blankets etc. became ditched after completely unloading and in consequence the blankets etc. of the Companies did not arrive until late in the evening.	A B
	4th		Training carried on as per training programme.	A.C.

Army Form C. 2118.

WAR DIARY
or
INTELLIGENCE SUMMARY.
(Erase heading not required.)

NOVEMBER 1918

Place	Date	Hour	Summary of Events and Information	Remarks and references to Appendices
PETIT AUDENARDE	4th		The Divisional General - Major Genl P.C.B. Skinner C.M.G., D.S.O., visited the Battalion for the purpose of presenting Military Medals awarded for bravery during the operations on 8th/9th/9th. The Brigadier General visited the Battalion during the afternoon.	
	5th		Training carried on as per programme.	
	6th		Training carried on. Wet weather made this weather difficult	
			Warning Order received for a move to forward area and issued to Companies.	
	7th		Training carried on.	
		2.30 p.m	At Brigade Headquarters. Commanding Officers conference at EVREGNIES	
		5.30	Company Commanders Conference held at Battalion Headquarters. Orders for move received late in evening.	
	8th		Preparations for move to DOTTIGNIES	E
DOTTIGNIES			The Battalion moved off at 13.30 hrs, arriving in billets at DOTTIGNIES by 16.00 hrs.	

WAR DIARY
INTELLIGENCE SUMMARY.

(Erase heading not required.)

Army Form C. 2118.

NOVEMBER 1918.

Place	Date	Hour	Summary of Events and Information	Remarks and references to Appendices
DOTTIGNIES	8th		Warning order to be ready to move at 30 minutes notice received.	
	9th	5.10pm	Warning order for move to HELCHIN received and issued to Companies.	F
		0700	Orders received for move HELCHIN. Parties sent forward to reconnoitre.	
HELCHIN		0845	Two companies moved forward.	G
		11.50	Message received from forward Companies. Remainder of Battalion moved to HELCHIN.	
			Battalion accommodated in billets and settled down for night.	
	10th	01.00	Warning order received to move to WARCOING.	
		03.00	Definite instructions issued [?] Companies for move to WARCOING.	H
		09.30	Battalion moved from HELCHIN. Transport moved separately. Billets difficult to find. Battalion settled down by 13.30 hrs.	
		1pm	Company Commanders Conference reworks on craters.	
		14.00	Half the Battalion went to work E. of L'ESCAUT filling in craters and clearing roads.	
		17.30	Working parties returned.	

WAR DIARY
INTELLIGENCE SUMMARY

Army Form C. 2118.

NOVEMBER 1918

Place	Date	Hour	Summary of Events and Information	Remarks and references to Appendices
WARCOING	10th	22.00	Battalion warned to be prepared to move at 4 hrs notice.	
	11th	08.00	Battalion proceeded to various points to get escort working on roads, craters, etc.	
		09.45	News received that Armistice had been signed. Hostilities cease at 11.00 hrs.	
		11.00	Hostilities cease.	
		14.30	Working parties returned.	
		15.00	Civilians returning to HELCHIN. Some difficulty about accommodation. Some wish to eject troops. Major Milne M.C. returned from leave to U.K. and assumed Command of the Battalion.	
	12th		Commanding Officers conference with Company Commanders re the proposed system of education during interval before demobilisation. Wire received containing some of the terms of the Armistice. Parties employed cleaning up civilian houses.	

WAR DIARY
INTELLIGENCE SUMMARY

Army Form C. 2118.

NOVEMBER 1918

Place	Date	Hour	Summary of Events and Information	Remarks and references to Appendices
WARCOING	12th		Conference of Battalion Staff Officers.	
	13th		Companies paraded for inspection, close order drill, physical training and a route march. Part of Battalion employed making a football ground for purpose of playing a Platoon tournament. One officer reinforcement joined during the morning. Civilians assisted in clearing up their houses.	
	14th		Scouts of the around two military graves and one D.C.M. to the Battalion for active operations in Sept 27/28. 1918 received. Battalion out working, repairing roads, filling in mine craters and shell holes. Commanding officer attended a Conference re-education at ROUBAIX. Party of one officer and four other ranks O.Rs sent off by the Travel B's table cart in a toreth light lattice in ROUBAIX during final week of December. Warning orders received for a move.	

WAR DIARY or INTELLIGENCE SUMMARY

Army Form C. 2118.

NOVEMBER 1918

Place	Date	Hour	Summary of Events and Information	Remarks and references to Appendices
MARCOING TOURCOING	15th	1000	Orders issued and preparations made to move to TOURCOING. Battalion moved off by motor-omnibus. Lorries carry blankets, greatcoats	I.
		1630	Arrived in LILLE. By 1630 hrs. three Companies and Battn. Hd.Qrs. entrained and one company and Transport on Western side of town. Men accommodated in factories. 75% have beds.	
	16th		One Company and 1 Transport moved to LILLE. He at remainder of Battalion. Palliasses provided for men without beds. Cleaning up, drill and route march included in parade for remainder of Battalion.	
			Party returned from D.R.C. Instructions received that Lieut. Colonel Richards, D.S.O. was here traced. Let and in likely to return to the Battalion Company commd. with	
	17th	1530	Brigadier Genl. visited the Battalion and inspected the Billets	
		0700	Party for Thanksgiving Service paraded. Service at 1000hrs.	

WAR DIARY
INTELLIGENCE SUMMARY

NOVEMBER 1918

Place	Date	Hour	Summary of Events and Information	Remarks and references to Appendices
TOURCOING	17th		Continue refitting and carrying on with kit inspections	
	18th	15.00	Voluntary Church Parade at 15.00 hrs in CIRQUE TOURCOING	
			Inspections and P.T. until 09.15 hrs	
		10.00	Battalion Parade. Reviewed drill Practice	
	19th		Washing feet. Battalion on line.	
			P.T. and Inspection of arms by Company Staff Sgts.	
	20th		Training interfered with considerably by a heavy fog	
			Company Commanders conference at 15.00 hrs.	
		19.30	Have received that Lieut-Colonel H. W. Richards drew on his way from the Brig. Reception Camp	
		21.45	Col. Richards arrived and resumed command of the Battalion	
	21st		Baths allotted to the Battalion. Every man bathed and received a clean change of undeclothing.	
		17.00	Company Commanders Conference at 17.00 hrs. re discipline	
			The Battalion team played the D.L. Suffolk Regt at football, losing by 3-0	

WAR DIARY
or
INTELLIGENCE SUMMARY.
(Erase heading not required.)

Army Form C. 2118.

November 1918

Place	Date	Hour	Summary of Events and Information	Remarks and references to Appendices
ROEUX	22nd	10.30	Training continued. Battalion parade at 10.30 hrs for ceremonial practice before Brigadier. Practice in afternoon. Commanding Officers Conference at Brigade before morning Parade.	
		D.45	The Battalion moved to the Brigade Parade Ground. The Brigade Practice was carried out successfully. Band returned from it Army School. Special orders issued to Battalion for kit inspection and cleaning it.	
	23rd	09.30	The Commanding Officer inspected the Band.	
		10.00	The Battalion paraded for ceremonial drill and practice for inspection and moved past.	
		14.30	Football match versus Brigade Headquarters. Game ended first 1/2 hour to right, the ends Score 1—1.	
	24th	09.30	R.C. Church parade.	
		10.30	Nonconformist Parade.	
		11.00	C of E Parade. The Band provided the music. Special orders issued re inspection suit	

WAR DIARY
or
INTELLIGENCE SUMMARY.
(Erase heading not required.)

Army Form C. 2118.

Place: FOUR CROSS ROADS
Month: November 1917

Date	Hour	Summary of Events and Information	Remarks and references to Appendices
25th		The Battalion moved to Brigade grounds for inspection by XV Corps Commander. The inspection was a success, and the Battalion marching and drill extremely well. The Battalion returned from the inspection.	I
26th	09.00	The Commanding Officer took Command of the Brigade. Company training. General Lewis Gun Seven days course commenced.	
	11.00	Battalion Parade practising ceremonial. A Brigade cross country run took place during the afternoon. Education scheme began to function. Several classes held during afternoon and evening.	
27th	Fog	Training as usual. Checking of stores & equipment commenced.	
	11.00	Battalion Parade. The Battalion played the 10th H.L.I. in the Brigade football competition during the afternoon, losing 3-2.	
28th		Parades cancelled owing to the wet weather, training cancelled.	

WAR DIARY
INTELLIGENCE SUMMARY

Army Form C. 2118.

Place	Date	Hour	Summary of Events and Information	Remarks and references to Appendices
TOURCOING	28th		in billets. The Commanding officer visited Companies and gave short lectures	havelersy L S.
			Stores & equipment checking continued	
	29th	0845	Training under Company arrangements	
		0945	The Brigadier General visited the Battalion Sports during the morning. Stores & equipment check-up continued.	
		1000	The Commanding Officer judged the Platoon Competition - one from each company competing. "C" Company's Platoon was judged so as to represent the Battalion in the Brigade Competition.	
	30th	10.15	Lecture to the lieutenant on "Recruiting and Demobilisation"	
		0845	Training under Company arrangements	
		10.00	Best company guards inspected & tested by Commanding Officer. Company Guard chosen to represent the Battalion in Brigade competition.	
		11.15	Battalion Parade for Battalion drill and Ceremonial.	

Rhebach Rehat 3 of Col.
Comdg. 2/5th Middlesex Regt.

MOVE ORDERS

WARNING ORDERS

1. The Battalion will move to ESTAMPUIS Area tomorrow.
   Order of march:- H.Q., "A" "B" Drums "C" "D"
   T.M. Section will parade with Headquarters.
   2. Platoons will move at 100 yards intervals.

2. Time of moving will be notified later.

3. **Billeting Parties**, as already detailed, will proceed in advance to take over billets. Advance parties of -- Division will arrive during the morning of November 3rd to take over present billets.

4. **Delivering of rations** will be notified later.

5. **BAGGAGE AND LORRY**.
   Baggage will be stacked as follows: by 0900 hours

   I. At Q.M.Stores. Blankets and Greatcoats of Headquarter Personnel. Headquarter Officers' Valises. Headquarter Mess Kit. Band Rifles, Packs and haversacks.
   II. At "A" & "B" Coys Headquarters. "A" & "B" Coys Blankets and Greatcoats. Company Stores. Company Mess Kit.
   III. At "C" & "D" Coys Headquarters. "C" & "D" Coys Blankets and Greatcoats. Coy Stores. Coy Mess Kit.

   O.C. each Company will detail 2 O.Rs to assist load the baggage. 1 O.R. will guard the company dump and the other O.R. will report to 2/Lieutenant H.N.TANNER at Q.M.Stores at 0900 hours. 2/Lieut: TANNER will utilise this party as a loading party for all the above dumps. One Lorry will be at the Q.M.Store at 0900 hours and will do three journeys, taking baggage as stated above (I, II, III.) Loading parties will travel on the lorry which takes the baggage of their companies (i.e. "A" & "B" loading party of 2nd journey. "C" & "D" Loading party and 2/Lieut: TANNER on 3rd journey.)
   G.S.Wagons. No: 1 G.S.Wagon will be placed at the disposal of the Quartermaster.
   No: 2 G.S.Wagon will carry Officers' Valises (less H.Qrs) Orderly Room Stores and Canteen Stores.
   Greatcoats will be securely tied in bundles of 20.

   Particular attention is called to the above instructions in order that the baggage may be moved as easily as possible.

6. Vacated billets will be left scrupulously clean.

                        (sd) COLIN SHEE, Captain & Adjutant,
                            20th Battalion Middlesex Regiment.

DISTRIBUTION:-
"A" Company,	Intelligence Offr:	Trench Mortar Offr.
"B" Company,	Medical Officer.	A/R. S. M.
"C" Company,	Quartermaster.	War Diary.
"D" Company,	Transport Offr:	File.
Signal Officer.	Chaplin.	

War Diary.

A

MOVE ORDERS

WARNING ORDERS

1. The Battalion will move to ESTAMPUIS Area tomorrow,
   Order of march:- H.Q., "A" "B" Drums "C" "D"
   T.M. Section will parade with Headquarters.
   2. Platoons will move at 100 yards intervals.

2. Time of moving will be notified later.

3. Billeting Parties, as already detailed, will proceed in
   advance to take over billets. Advance parties of --
   Division will arrive during the morning of November
   3rd to take over present billets.

4. Delivering of rations will be notified later.

5. BAGGAGE AND LORRY.
   Baggage will be stacked as follows: by 0900 hours

   I. At Q.M.Stores. Blankets and Greatcoats of Headquarter
      Personnel. Headquarter Officers' Valises. Headquarter
      Mess Kit. Band Rifles, Packs and haversacks.
   II. At "A" & "B" Coys Headquarters. "A" & "B" Coys
       Blankets and Greatcoats. Company Stores. Company
       Mess Kit.
   III. At "C" & "D" Coys Headquarters. "C" & "D" Coys
        Blankets and Greatcoats. Coy Stores. Coy Mess Kit.

   O.C. each Company will detail 2 O.Rs to assist load the
   baggage. 1 O.R. will guard the company dump and the
   other O.R. will report to 2/Lieutenant H.N.TANNER at
   Q.M.Stores at 0900 hours. 2/Lieut: TANNER will utilise
   this party as a loading party for all the above dumps.
   One Lorry will be at the Q.M.Store at 0900 hours and will
   do three journeys, taking baggage as stated above (I, II,
   III.) Loading parties will travel on the lorry which
   takes the baggage of their companies (i.e. "A" & "B"
   loading party of 2nd journey. "C" & "D" Loading party
   and 2/Lieut: TANNER on 3rd journey.)
   G.S.Wagons. No: 1 G.S.Wagon will be placed at the disposal
   of the Quartermaster.
   No: 2 G.S.Wagon will carry Officers' Valises (less H.Qrs.)
   Orderly Room Stores and Canteen Stores.
   Greatcoats will be securely tied in bundles of 20.

   Particular attention is called to the above instructions
   in order that the baggage may be moved as easily as
   possible.

6. Vacated billets will be left scrupulously clean.

                    (sd) COLIN SMEE, Captain & Adjutant,
                         20th Battalion Middlesex Regiment.

DISTRIBUTION:-
    "A" Company,   Intelligence Offr: Trench Mortar Offr.
    "B" Company,   Medical Officer.   A/R.S.M.
    "C" Company,   Quartermaster.   War Diary.
    "D" Company,   Transport Offr: File.
    Signal Officer.   Chaplin.

War Diary.

B

MOVE ORDERS

The head of the column will pass the church at LUINGHE at 1000 hours.

    Reveille:- 0645.
    Breakfast:- 0730.
    Sick Parade will be held in
    new area at 1400 hours.

G.S. Wagon will collect Company Officers' Kits as follows:-

    "D" Company:- 0800 hours.
    "C" Company:- 0830 hours.
    "B" Company:- 0900 hours.
    "A" Company:- 0930 hours.

                           (sd) COLIN SYME, Captain & Adjt.,
                              20th Battalion, Middlesex Regt.

2-11-18.

Distribution:-

    As for WARNING ORDER.

20th Battalion Middlesex Regiment.

TRAINING PROGRAMME for week ending Nov: 11th, 1918.

Date.	"A" Coy.	"B" Coy.	"C" Coy.	"D" Coy.	Remarks.
Nov. 4th.	0830 - 0900. Company Commander's Inspection. 0900 - 1000 O.Cs Inspection. 1015 - 1045 Physical Trg. 1045 - 1200 Attack Formations. 1200 - 1250 Gas.	0900 - 1000 hrs. Close Order Drill. 1015 - 1045 " Trigger Pressing and aiming. 1045 - 1130 " Fire and movement and use of ground. 1130 - 1250. Artillery Formations.			Coys parade at full strength for O.Cs Inspection. Specialist Classes commence at 0900 daily.
Nov: 5th.	0830 - 0900 O.C.Coys Inspection. 0900 - 1000 Close Order Drill. 1015 - 1045 Trigger Pressing & aiming. 1045 - 1130 Fire & movement & use of ground. 1130 - 1250 Artillery Formns.	0900 - 1000 O.Cs Inspn: 1015 - 1250 Same as "A" for Nov 4th.	0830 - 1250. Company at disposal of O.C.Company.	0830 - 0900 O.C.Coys' Inspection. 0900 - 1250 Range.	Platoons not actually firing on Range get musketry instruction. Rapid loading, aiming snapping, fire orders and movement.
Nov 6th	0830 - 1250 Coy: at disposal of O.C. Company.	0830 - 0900 O.C.Company's Inspection. 0900 - 1250 Range.	0830 - 0900 O.C.Coys Inspection. 0900 - 1000 O.Cs Inspn: 1015 - 1250 Same as "A" for Nov 4th.	0830 - 1250. Company at disposal of O.C. Company.	Afternoons:- 2.15 - N.C.Os instructed by Platoon Commanders, in Map Reading and message writing on alternate days. 1415 - 1515 Organised Games.
Nov: 7th	0830 - 0900 O.C.Companys' Inspection. 0900-0930 Range	0830 - 1250 Company at disposal of O.C. Coy.	0830 - 0900 O.C.Coys' Inspn: 0900 - 1100 Patrol Formations. 1100 - 1200 Close Order Drill. 1200/1250 Gas.	0830 - 0900 O.C. Coys Inspection. 0900 - 1000 O.Cs Inspn: 1015 - 1250 Same as "A" for Nov 4th.	
Nov 8th.	0830 - 0900 O.C. Companys' Inspection. 0900 - 1250 Same as "C" for Nov 7th	0900 - 1250 Same as "C" for Nov 7th.	0900 - 1250 Range.	0900 - 1250 Same as "C" for Nov 7th.	
Nov: 9th.	0830 - 0930. 0945 - 1015. 1015 - 1250.	B A T T A L I O N P A R A D E. Physical Training. Attack Formations.			

(sd) R.J.LUCAS, 2/Lieutenant and A/Adjt., 20th Battalion Middlesex Regiment.

Bn: Middlesex Regiment

SECRET.   Operation Order No: 27.   Copy No: 15

Ref Shoot COURTRAI.1.   1/40,000.

1. The 43rd Infantry Brigade will relieve the 41st Infantry
   Brigade in the Line on the night November 8/9th, 1918.
   Relief to be complete by 0001 hours, 9th instant.

2. The Brigade boundaries will be as follows:-
   Northern Boundary:-   29/U.30.c. central - to U.8.b.2.8.-
                         thence S.W. through T.17. central to
                         Northern outskirts of HERSEAUX.
   Southern Boundary:-   37/C.15.c.8.5. - B.18.c.6.8. (Bridge
                         inclus) - along south bank of canal,
                         to B.23.a.8.5. - thence along N. Bank
                         of canal.
   Inter-Battalion Boundary:- C.4.a.90.20. - U.28.a.10.00
                         thence N.W. along Road to U.21.d.20.00.
                         - U.19.c.00.00 Road inclusive to
                         Left Battalion.

3. Advance Parties. Advance parties of one Officer and one
   N.C.O. per Company and B.HQ. will leave present billets
   at 0800 hrs., and proceed to DOTTIGNIES, there taking
   over from companies of corresponding letter.

4. The Battalion will move with First Line Transport in the
   following order:- HQ., "B","A","D","C", Head of column
   passing B.7.d.40.70. at 1330 hours. 200 yards interval
   between platoons and each six vehicles will be maintained.
   Cookers will proceed immediately in rear of leading
   platoon of each company. Steel Helmets will be worn.
   Jerkins and Haversacks will be carried.

5. One Lorry per Battalion will report to present B.HQ. at
   about 1500 hours. This Lorry may make two journeys.

6. BAGGAGE. Officers' Valises, Blankets in Rolls of ten, and
   Company Stores will be stacked outside Bn: H.Qrs and Coy:
   H.Qrs., by 0900. One G.S.Wagon and one Limber will collect
   for "A" and "B" Companies and 1 G.S. Wagon and one Limber
   for "C" and "D" Companies. HQ. Officers' Valises will
   complete the loads for those two limbers. These vehicles
   will proceed in the morning to DOTTIGNIES under arrangements
   made by the Transport Officer and unload at places to be
   selected by the advance parties. The two G.S.Wagons will
   return and one will collect Orderly Room Stores, H.Q.
   Blankets, Greatcoats and cooking utensils. The other G.S.
   Wagon will report to Q.M. Stores. The two limbers will
   return to Transport Lines.
   The Mess Cart will collect Mess Kit of H.Q. and Coys., as
   under:-   "C", "D", H.Q., "B", "A", commencing at "C"
   Company at 1230 hours. Company greatcoats will be rolled
   in bundles of ten and stacked under archway by headquarter
   guard. These will be man-handled to this dump. One man
   per company will be left to load these and look after his
   own Company's coats. These will be collected by a Lorry
   at about 1500 hours. The Maltese Cart will report to the
   R.A.P. at 0900 hours and proceed with the 2 G.S.Wagons and
   two limbers already detailed. On return from DOTTIGNIES,
   it will report to Corporal TRUSS to collect the mail.

7. Transport Lines and Quartermaster's Stores in the forward
   Area will be located at T.28.c.4.9. Transport must
   arrive in new Transport Lines by 1300 hours on 8th inst.

(Continued)

Operation Order No: 27. (Sheet 2)

8. **RATIONS.** Rations for consumption on November 9th will be delivered to present Transport Lines on morning of Nov: 8th. A guide will report to the Quartermaster at 0900 to conduct those wagons to the new location. The Duty Company will arrange for a guard of one N.C.O. and 3 men to accompany those wagons. They will unload and guard the rations at the new Quartermaster's Stores.

9. Completion of Company reliefs will be reported to B.H.Q. by wire in the code of Company Commander's Name.

10. Brigade Headquarters will close at EVREGNIES at 2100 hrs., and will open at DOTTIGNIES (T.29.c.5.4.) on arrival.

11. Personnel as already arranged for the D.R.O. will be under the Command of Lieutenant A.J.JOHNSON. Kits of all ranks of this party must not be collected with the kits already detailed. Orders for this party will be issued later to Lieutenant A.J.JOHNSON. Band Instruments will be taken by this party to the D.R.O.

12. Lieutenant A.J.GASS will relieve the Town Major of DOTTIGNIES. He will report to the Headquarters of the 41st Infantry Brigade at 1000 hours, November, 8th.

13. The duty Company will relieve the guard at Brigade H.Qrs in DOTTIGNIES by Gas guard of 1 N.C.O. and 3 men to report immediately on arrival of battalion in billets.

14. Quartermaster will make arrangements to ration the Divl: Burial Party (strength 23 all ranks) from Nov: 10th incl.

15. **Area Stores.** Area Stores, S.O.S. Rockets and Air Photos will be taken over by advance parties.

         (sd) R.J.LUCAS, 2/Lieutenant & A/Adjt.,
         20th Battn: Middlesex Regiment.

DISTRIBUTION.

  Copy No: 1. O.C. "A" Company.
      2.   "B" Company.
      3.   "C" Company.
      4.   "D" Company.
      5. Adjutant.
      6. Second in Command.
      7. Quartermaster.
      8. Transport Officer.
      9. Signals.
     10. Medical Officer.
     11. Lieutenant A.J.JOHNSON.
     12. Lieutenant A.J.GASS.
     13. Offr i/c T.M.Section.
     14. R.S.M.
     15. War Diary.
     16. File.

C.O. 2/c I.O. M.O. Qm.
Signals All Companies R.S.m.

F

Warning Order

The Battalion will move forward
to be clear of present billets
by 0800 hours.

Enemy has gone. F.O.B.U. are
going across now. 2 Coys
of R.E.s are across.

Men will have breakfast
before moving.

(sd) R J Lucas
2/Lieut
Adjt
9/4/18
20" Manch Rgt

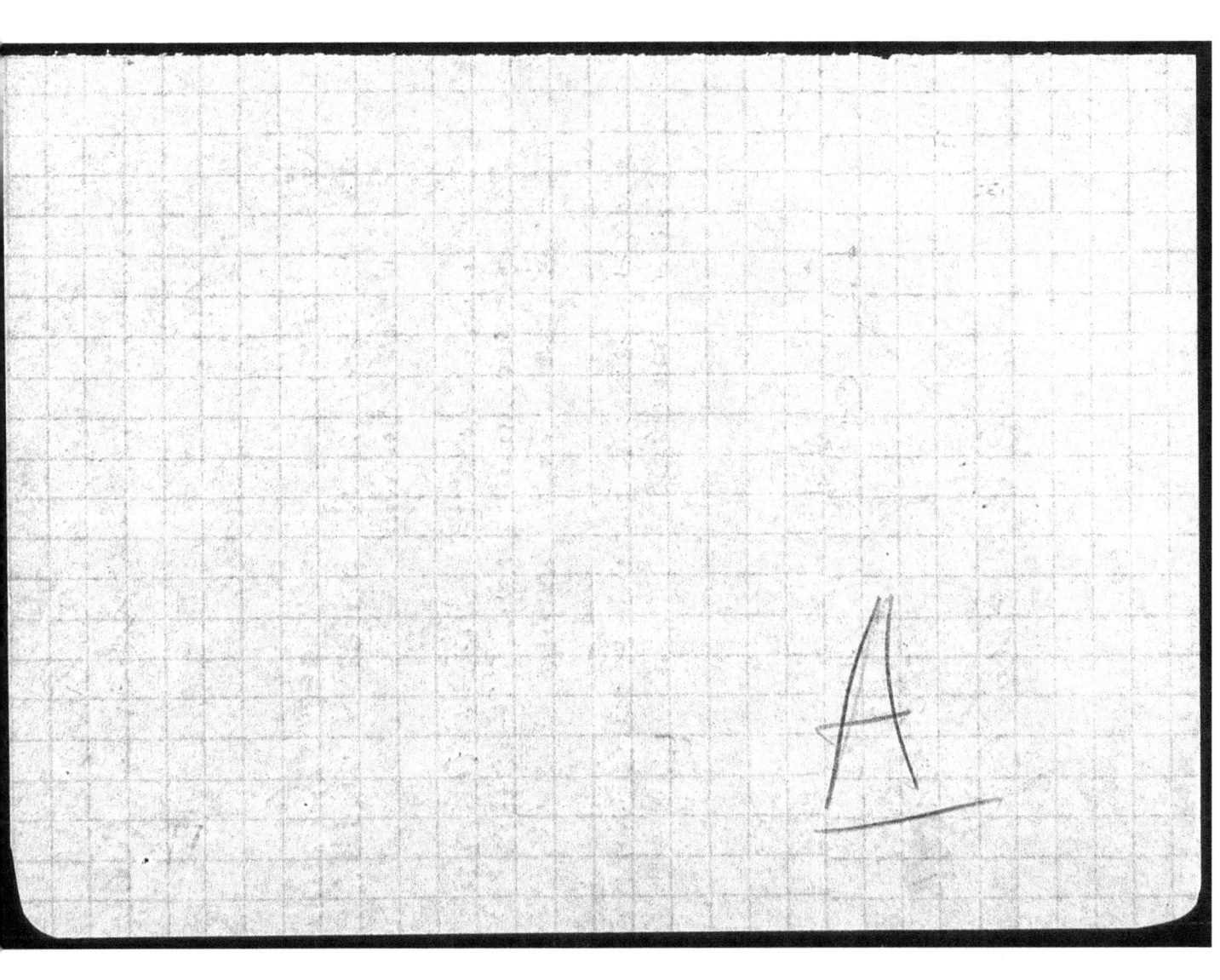

Operation Order No. 28

Ref. Sheet 37.   G.

1. The Battalion will move at 0845 hours to HELCHIN.
2. ~~The Battalion~~
2. Formation. Companies in Artillery formation of platoons in worms at 200 yards interval and distance.
3. Order of Battle. "A" Coy Right Front. "C" Coy. Left Front. "B" Right Support. "D" Left Support.
4. "A" & "C" Coys will move off ~~at 0800 hours~~ & be clear of DOTTIGNIES by 0845 hours. "B" & "D" Coys will stand fast & await further orders.
5. Batn. HQrs. will remain at present location for the present.

6. Transport as already arranged with Coys.

9/11/18

Operation Order
No. 29.   H
Ref. Sheet: COURTRAI 1/40,000.

<u>1</u> The Battalion will move
to WARCOING via ESPIERRES
in following order.
   H.Q. D C A B.   Head of
column to pass X Roads in
HELCHIN (U 29 c 27) at 10.00.

<u>11</u> Billeting parties of 1 officer
& 1 N.C.O. per Coy. & H.Q. will
report to LT. E. C. P. WILLIAMS.
M.C. at 07.45 hrs. at X Roads
at U 29 c 27. This party
will report to the Staff
Captain at 09.15 at X Roads
WARCOING C 20 a 4.7.

<u>3</u> Platoons will move at
100 yds. interval. Lewis Gun
limbers & cookers will be
in rear of 1st & 2nd platoons

2

3. cont'd
respectively of each Coy.
Trench mortar limber will move
in rear of C. Coy's last platoon.

4. Remainder of the transport
will move under orders of
the B.T.O. & will arrive in
new area by 12.00.

5. The 43 Inf. Bde. are responsible for clearing roads E. of
L'ESCAUT. The following
mines & craters will be attended
to by this Battn.
    C. 10 d 6.0.
    C. 17 d 3.9
    D. 20 d 5.9.
Tasks will be allotted to Coys.
on arrival in new area.
The Transport Officer will
draw the following tools from
the Bde. Mobile Reserve,
immediately on arrival at

5 cont'd   3
    new area.
        Up to 160 shovels and
        50 picks.
    There will be dumped at
    the O.R. trailer stores together
    with all tools carried as a
    mobile reserve on first line
    transport.
        The 2nd in command
    will go forward at 0830 hours
    to reconnoitre the above three
    points & any roads E. of L'Escaut
    over which the Coys will have
    to pass to reach these points.
    He will report back to B.H.Q.
    by 12.30 in new area in
    order to allot tasks to Coys.
        The Transport Officer will
    have the charges & groom
    (mounted) of 2ft ready at
    present Bn H.Q. by 0815 hours.
6. Dinners will be served immediately
    on arrival in billets.

2.

1. Coys will be prepared to send out working parties during the afternoon of 10 inst.

2. Coy Comdrs will report at BHQ personally the arrival of their Coys in billets, & await to attend Commanding Officers Conference re work.

P Lucas
a/adjt.
2o Middlesex Regt.

10/11/18

A — A/g OH
B — Q.M.
C — M.O.
D — R.S.M.
¼ Y
a/jt
T.O.

20th Battalion Middlesex Regiment.

Operation Order No. 28.

Reference Sheet 37 1/40,000.

(a)
    Reveille :- 0600.
    Sick parade:- 0630.
    Breakfast:- 0700.

1. The Battalion will move with First Line Transport to Western TOURCOING in the following order,
    H.Q. "D" "C" "B" "A" Head of column passing ForkRoads at C.14.c.2.9. at 10.00 hours.
  (b) 100 yards interval between Companies, usual intervals between transport. Head of Transport 100 yards in rear of last platoon of "A" Company.
  (c) Dress. Service Caps.
          Jerkins in packs.
  (d) Dinners will be cooked on route, Cookers will proceed with transport.

2. ROUTE. EVREGNIES - PETIT AUDENARDE - WATTRELOS.

3. ADVANCE PARTIES. 2/Lieutenant C.H. MONTAGUE will proceed with the Staff Captain by car leaving B.H.Q., at 0845 hours. Billeting parties of one N.C.O. per Company, Transport, Q.M., and H.Q., will report to Sergt. Johnson at B.H.Q., at 0725 hours. This party under the Command of Sergt Johnson will proceed by bicycle, reporting with bicycles, to the Staff Captain at 0930 hours at the HOTEL DE VILLE, TOURCOING. The N.C.O. from the Q.M.Stores will meet the supply wagons at 1400 hours at the HOTEL DE VILLE, TOURCOING, and guide them to the new Q.M.Stores.

4. BAGGAGE.
  i. 2 Lorries will collect Company baggage as under.
    One lorry will collect A & B Companies blankets (in bundles of 10) and sandbags (containing Great coats and Haversacks), Company Stores, Officers Valises and Mess Kit starting at "A" Company at 0815 hours.
    Second lorry will collect for C and D Companies as above starting at "D" Company at 0815.
  ii One G.S.Wagon will carry the Q.M.Stores.
    One G.S.Wagon and Mess Cart will report to B.H.Q., at 0900 hours. The G.S.Wagon will carry H.Q.Blankets (in bundles of 10), Great Coats and Haversacks (in sandbags) Headquarters Cooking utensils H.Q.Officers Valises, and Mess Kit.
    The Mess Cart will carry Orderly Room Stores.
  iii Headquarter Blankets, Greatcoats, etc. will be stacked under the archway behind the Guard ready for loading at 0900 hours. Companies will arrange for central Dumps of their blankets and Greatcoats to be ready for loading at the above times.

5. Sick will be collected by the 44 F.A. at 0900.
6. Brigade H.Q. will close at TOURCOING at 1000 hours and will open at TOURCOING.
7. Company Commanders will report as soon as possible, the arrival of their Companies in Billets by wiring to B.H.Q., the name of the Company Commander concerned.
8. O.C.Companies and the R.S.M. for Headquarters will forward to Orderly Room by 1900 hours 16th inst a complete list of all Billets (in duplicate) in the new area occupied by them in accordance with pro forma below.

Billet.		Accommodation.			Remarks*
Name of Street	No of Billet.	Officers	O.R.	Horses.	

* To be stated in column of remarks if available for Officers Mess, Offices, Aid Post, Q.M.Stores etc.

(sd) R.J.Lucas, 2/Lieut: and A/Adjt:
20th Battalion Middlesex Regiment.

15-11-18.
Issued 0200.

War Diary
J

20th Battalion, Middlesex Regiment.

ORDERS FOR PARADE FOR CORPS
COMMANDER'S INSPECTION.

1. The Battalion, plus 1st Line Transport, will march to the Parade Ground in S.13.d. in the following order:-
    Band, "A", "B", "C", "D", Transport.
    Head of the column passing Headquarter Mess at 0815 hrs.

2. The following will report to the R.S.M. outside the Orderly Room at 0750 hours.
    (a) 1 marker per platoon.
    (b) 1 signaller from H.Qrs with one white flag.
    This party will report to the Brigade Major at 0900 hours at the entrance to No: 10 C.C.S.

3. Personnel from Headquarters and each Company to be left off will be as already detailed - in addition the Pioneers will not parade.

4. Dress:- Musketry Order, as already shown to Coy Sgt Majors.

5. The following additional instructions are issued:-
    (a) Warrant Officers will not carry sticks.
    (b) Water-proof sheets will not be carried.
    (c) The distance between companies when formed up in column for the march past will be 5 paces.
    (d) The distances during the march past will be 40 paces between companies and 60 paces between Battalions.
    (e) Bands, in passing through troops of or the inspection, will take each the shortest route instead of passing each on the left of its Battalion.
    (f) The General Salute will be blown on both occasions by the 12th Suffolk Regt Buglers only.

6. Company Commanders will notify this office by 1800 hours today, the exact frontage of their leading platoons when drawn up in Mass.

7. Company Parade States, showing numbers of Officers and Other Ranks on parade, will be rendered by 2000 hours today. The Transport Officer will render a parade state showing number of Other Ranks, Animals and Vehicles. The Sergeant-Drummer to render a parade state for the Drums and Band by 2000 hours. Company Parade States will not include Transport, Band or Drums.

8. Grooms should, during the parade, wait in readiness, 30 yards in rear of the **right** flag of the Saluting Base.

(sd) R.J.LUCAS, 2/Lieutenant
and A/Adjutant,
20th Battalion, Middlesex Regiment.

Issue at 1600 hrs,
24-11-18.

WAR DIARY.

20th Batt. MIDDLESEX Regt.

DECEMBER 1916

Army Form C. 2118.

WAR DIARY
or
INTELLIGENCE SUMMARY.
(Erase heading not required.)

Instructions regarding War Diaries and Intelligence Summaries are contained in F. S. Regs., Part II. and the Staff Manual respectively. Title pages will be prepared in manuscript.

DECEMBER 1918.

Place	Date	Hour	Summary of Events and Information	Remarks and references to Appendices
TOURCOING	DEC 1st		Church Parades for all Denominations at various times during the morning.	
	2nd	08.30	Pt. and Barrack Rifle inspection and Medical inspection.	
		09.15	Battalion Parade. The Battalion went on route march to Outskirts of ROUBAIX along East side of Canal returning alongside W. side of Canal. Lecture on Otflocators during the morning to percentage of all ranks	
	3rd	8.30	Battalion Theme started. The Battalion bathed.	
		08.30	Working party supplied to unloaded coal. Classes of Illiterates and Company Training carried on during intervals of Battn. Adjt Torch light Tattoo held in Square at ROUBAIX not as interesting as one expected.	
	4th	08.45	Company Training continued Arms inspection	

A6945 Wt W14422/M1160 35,000 12/16 D. D. & L. Forms/C./2118/14.

Army Form C. 2118.

WAR DIARY
or
INTELLIGENCE SUMMARY.
(Erase heading not required.)

DECEMBER 1918

Place	Date	Hour	Summary of Events and Information	Remarks and references to Appendices
TOURCOING	4th	11.30 a.m.	Battalion Parade. Wet weather made the parade ground very muddy. Divisional Boxing Competition commenced in the Cine Cinema at 11.30 a.m.	
	5th		Commander Company went half. Battalion parade cancelled owing to weather and numbers of men off parade for various entertainments.	
		11.30	Brigade Rugger XV played the R.E. A. and lost 7-5. Orders issued re practice for Army Commanders Inspection. Battery Contests during afternoon.	
	6th	8.45 a.m.	Battalion Paraded and moved off to ground for practice Inspection. Finals of boxing competition. Battalion candidates marched out after Supper. F.M.K. The Adjutant Capt. B. Snee M.C. returned from 30 days leave.	A.

A6945 Wt. W14422/M1160 35,000 12/16 (D. D. & L. Forms/C./2118/14.

Army Form C. 2118.

WAR DIARY
or
INTELLIGENCE SUMMARY.
(Erase heading not required.)

DECEMBER 1918.

Instructions regarding War Diaries and Intelligence Summaries are contained in F. S. Regs., Part II. and the Staff Manual respectively. Title pages will be prepared in manuscript.

Place	Date	Hour	Summary of Events and Information	Remarks and references to Appendices
TOURCOING	Dec. 7th	7.845	Colour kills and kit inspection by the Commanding Officer.	
		07.30	Football match (competition) versus R.E's. Result 2 – 0. Volunteer party went to have the Park for the day, who were busy on tidying up LILLE	
	8th	07.30	Battalion Concert Party gave its first performance Godshow. Sunday Services during morning. Football competition continued. Platoon Football Competition continued. Brigade Rugby XV played Australian Heavy Artillery and lost.	
	9th	8.45	Company Training as usual.	
		11.00	Battalion Parade. S.A.A. handed in to Army.	
	10th	8.10	Companies paraded and prepared to move off to be inspected by the Army Commander, at 11.00 very wet. Inspection was cut short owing to wet weather	
	11th	8.45	Company training as usual. Volunteers inoculated.	

WAR DIARY
or
INTELLIGENCE SUMMARY.
(Erase heading not required.)

Army Form C. 2118.

December 1918.

Place	Date	Hour	Summary of Events and Information	Remarks and references to Appendices
TOURCOING	11th	cont.	with the resources to counter effects of the epidemic of influenza. Recline or "flying" at the Cirque Cinema.	
	12th		Prepare watching Brigade Football Competition scratched. Company training. Circulation. Count of Company Rd & LG report on loss of bicycles supposed stolen.	
	13th		Lecture on "Demobilization". Platoon and Guard Competition. Our Platoon both secured places. The Guards bed and kadir parade again in the 14th. Guard Competition.	
	14th		Companies carried on training. Platoon and RT. The football team played the 16th Middlesex team in the Divisional competition and lost 3-0.	
	15th		Church Parade for all. Demobilization. Demobilization.	

A6945 Wt.W14427/M1160 35,000 12/16 D. D. & L. Forms/C./2118/14.

WAR DIARY
or
INTELLIGENCE SUMMARY.

Army Form C. 2118.

December 1918

Place	Date	Hour	Summary of Events and Information	Remarks and references to Appendices
TOURCOING	15th ctd.	9.30	Company continued. Photograph of the Platoon was taken.	
			The Brigade Rugby team played the R.G.A. of DOUVRIN and lost heavily. Several interplatoon matches played off.	
	16th	845	Company Inspection followed by Platoon drill.	
		1100	Battalion Parade for ceremonial drill.	
	17th	845	Company Parades followed by Battalion Parade. Baths during afternoon for "D" Company. Lecture on "Alsace-Lorraine" in Cinema Cinema.	
	18th	8.30	Company Parades. Drill and Guard mounting Inspection by M.D. for Secuties. A+C Companies bathed at Divisional Bath.	
	19th	8.30	Company Parades as usual. "B" Company inoculated with new vaccine for prevention of ill-effects of epidemic influenza. No Ill- platoon matched played in afternoon.	

Army Form C. 2118.

WAR DIARY
or
INTELLIGENCE SUMMARY. DECEMBER 1918
(Erase heading not required.)

Instructions regarding War Diaries and Intelligence Summaries are contained in F. S. Regs., Part II. and the Staff Manual respectively. Title pages will be prepared in manuscript.

Place	Date	Hour	Summary of Events and Information	Remarks and references to Appendices
TOURCOING	20th	8.30	Usual Company parades. Inter-platoon football matches played during afternoon. Prize offered for best decorated Dining Room in Division.	
	21st	8.45	Company parades for inspection and drill	
		10.60	Battalion Parade & route march	
		14.00	Test match for purpose of picking Battalion team.	
		14.00	Inter War teams practice	
	22nd		Church Parades for all denominations.	
	23rd	8.30	Company parades of inspection and drill and P.T.	
			Match v. 11th Field Ambulance cancelled	
			Parades on 22nd & 23rd	
	24th		did with mass by R.C.	
			The other units with the Brigade were invited late in the evening by the Battalion Coal Party. There were much appreciated. The Party found the work very arduous.	

WAR DIARY
INTELLIGENCE SUMMARY
(Erase heading not required)

Army Form C. 2118.

DECEMBER 1918.

Place	Date	Hour	Summary of Events and Information	Remarks and references to Appendices
TOURCOING	25th	11.00	Divine Service inspected by the Brigadier-General. "B" Company took the prize for the best decorated room.	
		13.00	Men had their Christmas dinner.	
		15.00	The "Scroungers" – the Battalion Dramatic Society – gave their first performance. It was a great success.	
		18.00	The Sgts. had their Christmas dinner.	
		20.00	The Officers sat down to dinner. The evening passed off quietly.	
	26th	11.00	The Sgts. and Officers played football. The match resulted in a win for the Officers after a hotly contested game. Score 2–1.	
	27th	8.30	Paraded under Company arrangements.	
		10.00	Lecture on "Agriculture". The Cirque Cinema. Football match v/ Argyle and Sutherland Highlanders abandoned owing to the wet.	
	28th		Paraded as on 27th inst. Parties RAC. Captains rather	
	29th		Church Services for all Denominations except C of E – there being no C of E Padre available – and the wet day.	

WAR DIARY
INTELLIGENCE SUMMARY.
(Erase heading not required.)

Army Form C. 2118.

DECEMBER 1918

Place	Date	Hour	Summary of Events and Information	Remarks and references to Appendices
TOURCOING	30th		Match Argyle v Sutherlands resulting in a loss 2-3 to 4.5. Ingofraor v 10th M.I. resulted in a draw 2 apiece for M.I. Information received as to interchange of Brigade Areas on Jan 3rd & 4th. This Battalion relieving 8th Bn relieves Jany 29th D.L.I. who up to the present have been at AU JARDON in the BOIS VERT CHATEAU near BONDUES - Commanding Officer visited their area - Billets as King Like as good as these but much entertainment for the men - Commencement of arranging for extra entertainments in all held in The Battalion.	
	31st		Preparation for GOC's Inspection of the Battalion by Companies in different dress to take place tomorrow Jan 1st. For Officers of this Battalion played 4 Officers of 10th M.I. at Badminton Singles & Ping-Pong in the afternoon - Resulting in Middlesex winning the Singles & all the Badminton (2 Singles & 2 Doubles) losing 4 games of Ping-pong, their winning a dinner of the M.I.; Battalion bathed in Municipal Baths.	
	31st 23:59 1/1/19 00:01		A merry New Year all round	

Mychelvolle Richards Lt Col
Comdg 20th Middlesex Regt

ARMY COMMANDER'S INSPECTION. (Practice).

War Diary
A

1. There will be a Practice parade tomorrow for the Army Commander's Inspection as per 18th Div: G.S. 1843.

2. Companies will parade at 0845 hrs. The Battalion will move off in the following order:- Band & Drums, "A" "B" "C" "D", Transport; the head of the column will pass 38/F.11.a.5.2. at 0915 hrs. Intervals of 10 yards between Companies and Transport will be maintained. Units will halt at 1000 hrs for ten minutes. No other halt will be allowed before reaching the parade ground. Company Commanders must be careful to have the right flank of their Companies leading. Four Company L.Gun Limbers will parade loaded as for the Inspection by the Corps Commander. Feeds will be taken for all horses.

3. Companies will parade at equal strength and will be sized. To do this the following adjustments are necessary:- "C", 5 files to "B". "D", 7 files to "B". These files from "C" Company will be in rear platoon of "B" Company. Platoons will be of equal strength. The following personnel only will be left off parade:- The R.S.M. must ensure that all H.Q. Personnel not detailed below, are paraded with their companies.

   (a) <u>HEADQUARTERS</u>. Offrs' Mess Staff.   Q.M.Stores Personnel.
                            Quarter Guard.   Battalion Police. (to guard
                            Canteen Personnel.   Sanitary Squad. Bn: billets)
                            Aid Post Personnel.   3 Servants.
                            4 Signallers.   4 Runners.
                            O.R. Staff.   Educational Staff.
                            Pioneers.   2 Cooks.
                            Transport personnel not required with L.G.Limbers
                            and Mess Cart.

   (b) <u>COMPANIES</u>.   4 Cooks.   1 Billet Orderly.
                            2 Servants.   C.Q.M.S.

   Unless special orders to the contrary are issued, the Duty Company will not find the usual fatigue parties for:-
   (1) No: 1 Area Commandant.   (1 N.C.O. & 10 men)
   (2) No: 8 C.C.S.   (1 N.C.O. & 20 men.)
   (3) Sanitary Duties.   (1 N.C.O. and 4 men).

4. <u>DRESS</u>. Drill Order. Waterproof sheets will be carried, rolled and strapped on belts. Company Commanders will be mounted - all dismounted officers will wear puttees. No sticks will be carried. Haversack rations will be carried. It is suggested that these might be carried in the ground sheet.

5. <u>LEWIS GUNS</u>. On arriving on the Parade Ground, and forming up, the Nos: 1 of each company will unload their guns and fall in with them in the supernumerary rank. Guns will be carried at the slope on the left shoulder during the march past - at all other times they will be held at the 'Order'.

6. One Right Guide per Company and Trench Mortar Section will report to the Brigade Major in rear of the 12th Suffolk Regiment immediately the Army Commander (probably represented by the Divisional Commander) has ridden round the troops and the order "Form Fours - Right" has been given.

7. <u>ADVANCE IN REVIEW ORDER</u>. The Divisional Commander will give the order "The Division will Advance in Review Order". After a slight pause, a "G" will be sounded on a bugle. All troops will step off when the "G" is sounded. A Second "G" will be sounded for the halt.

8. One marker per Company and one for T.M. Section will report to Sergt JOHNSON outside the Orderly Room at 0900 hrs. They will proceed independently to the Parade Ground and report to a Divisional Staff Officer, at 1030 hrs.

(Sd) R.J.LUCAS, 2/Lieutenant & A/Adjutant,
20th Battn: Middlesex Regiment.

5-12-18.

War Diary

20th Battalion Middlesex Regt.

January 1919

Army Form C. 2118.

WAR DIARY
or
INTELLIGENCE SUMMARY.

(Erase heading not required.)

Place	Date	Hour	Summary of Events and Information	Remarks and references to Appendices

Instructions regarding War Diaries and Intelligence Summaries are contained in F. S. Regs., Part II, and the Staff Manual respectively. Title pages will be prepared in manuscript.

A6945 Wt. W14425/M1160 35,000 12/16 D. D. & L. Forms/C./2118/14.

Army Form C. 2118.

WAR DIARY
or
INTELLIGENCE SUMMARY.   JANUARY 1919.
(Erase heading not required.)

Instructions regarding War Diaries and Intelligence Summaries are contained in F. S. Regs., Part II. and the Staff Manual respectively. Title pages will be prepared in manuscript.

Place	Date	Hour	Summary of Events and Information	Remarks and references to Appendices
TOURCOING	1st		GOC's Inspection - A + B Companies Kit Inspection. C Company Arms drill - D Company Full marching order. All quite satisfactory. Information received that move will not take place on Jan 3rd - 4th. On Saturday our opponents in the match with 46th Bde R.F.A. Scratched. So a paper chase was held in place.	
	2nd		Preparation for move to BONDUES. Orderly 29th O.B.L.I. Billeting party 50R demobilized sent in advance & a similar party received. 30R demobilized.	
BONDUES	3rd	10:00	Marched to BONDUES. Arrived in Billets 12 noon. Accommodation A.	
(All Jan Bath)			Very poor 1st. Kt. for officers, mens, also billets not very clean. Troops paid. Shortage of Paillasses tried.	
	4th		Work on billets all day. A tremendous amount of work needed to make them at all comfortable. Agricultural Company moved to Company Billets vacated by 41 Agricultural Company. Remainder of Brigade moved into this area. 3rd Rounds Divisional League played against 47th Adv. R.F.A. Result 3-1 for the Battalion.	
	5th		Very wet day. Only R.C. Services held as no other Chaplain's available. 2 OR demobilized.	

WARD DIARY
INTELLIGENCE SUMMARY.
(Erase heading not required.)

Army Form C. 2118.

JANUARY 1919.

Place	Date	Hour	Summary of Events and Information	Remarks and references to Appendices
BONQUES.	6th		Training Parades reduced to System of 2 Battalion Parades a week Wednesdays & Saturdays. The short days under Company arrangements from 9-12, for PT games, ½ Order or musketry etc as may be. Board, Kit Inspections etc on Education Classes everyday except Weds & Saturdays. 1 OR Demobilized	B.
	7th		Normal day. Baths for all except B Company at ½ Headquarters. Lectures on "War Causes & War Issues." All Ranks assembled. Audit of all accounts of this Battalion — everything satisfactory. 4 Demobilized (OR)	
	8th		Normal Day. 1 OR Demobilized.	
	9th		Normal. Scheme whereby men & officers could be demobilized whilst on leave cancelled	
	10th		Normal. B Company & remainder of HQ bathed.	
	11th		Normal. Authority given for demolition of German huts & this producing badly needed firewood, wood for Officers to work on, & depriving the Military Police of Cases, criminal for demobilization Government property which was of no value. 1 OR Demobilized to shortleave 1/1/19 (A/S Buley) 1 OR & 8 OR Demobilized	

WAR DIARY
INTELLIGENCE SUMMARY
(Erase heading not required.)

Army Form C. 2118.

JANUARY 1919

Place	Date	Hour	Summary of Events and Information	Remarks and references to Appendices
BONDUES	12/15		Normal. 14th HEADEN proceeded on Senior Officers Course at Aldershot, from leave to UK. 14496 Pte. A. MITCHELL awarded Belgian Croix de Guerre for devotion to duty & gallantry on Sept 28th 1918. Divisional League for choosing Football Teams for Army Competition disbanded & teams selected by a committee. 10 R Dem: Dilutees.	
	13/15		Normal. Lectures on Demobilization given to the men. 40 R Dem: Dilutees. A Whist Drive for 32 men per Company held at 18.00hrs. Entrance fee 50 Centimes & 4 prizes given. Much enjoyed by all the men.	
	14/15		Normal. Re-enlistment men sworn in. 2 30 custom is provided to take men into TOURCOING to see Lady Blanic's performance of the MOTHUSC. A large party in strain from the transport sent to Staff Horse Allock, Coys at Camp at TOURCOING.	
	15/15		Normal.	
	16/15		Normal. 3 mon transport men sent away. Very difficult not to handle 1st few transport — Veterinary Board on all horses. Lecture by Rev T.P. IOAKIMUS on "Imperial History".	
	17/15		Normal. 11 or 12 Enlistment men sworn in. Our Company Baked.	

Army Form C. 2118.

WAR DIARY
or
INTELLIGENCE SUMMARY.
(Erase heading not required.)

January 1919.

Place	Date	Hour	Summary of Events and Information	Remarks and references to Appendices
BONDUES	18th		Normal. Kit inspections. 2 O.R. demobilized	
	19th		Church Services for all denominations. 2 O.R. demobilized.	
	20th		Normal. 1 Officer & 20 O.R. demobilized. Two American teams from U.S. Army gave a demonstration in Basket Ball at 14.30 hrs at ROUBAIX. 2 men per Company sent.	
	21st		Selection of posts for presentation of Colours by Corps Commander on 25 inst at ROUBAIX. After many contradictory orders, finally came down to a Colour party of 1 Officer 2 C.S.M's & 2 Corporals. A Guard of Honour of a Captain & 32 O.Ranks. 2/Lt H.M. Turner selected as Ensign. Capt S.G.H. Bower as O.C. Guard of Honour. Standard March past practised during the morning. Three companies & HQ bathed. Further enlistment men South in. 10 OR demobilized on leave 7.1.19 & 22 OR's demobilized	1 Officer has WO1 when AC
	22nd		Practice Presentation of Colours at TOURCOING for the Division. Lecture by Capt B.R.Q. Cook, Educators Officer "Geography 41000." 1 Officer & 9 O.R. Major I/c of Batt by Capt MC. 9th 19 OR demob. HRCS. 10R demob R to leave 9.1.19	
	23rd		Normal. Colour Party practised in Park.	
	24th		Normal. Service practice at TOURCOING for Colour presentation for the division. On Coy & BHQ bathed.	
	25th		COLOURS presented by the Corps Commander in the Square at ROUBAIX. The Battalion	

Army Form C. 2118.

WAR DIARY
or
INTELLIGENCE SUMMARY.
(Erase heading not required.)

January 1919.

Place	Date	Hour	Summary of Events and Information	Remarks and references to Appendices
BONDUES	25th/Jan		Band Sergeant conducted the massed bands of the Brigade. The Corps Commander had a speech after the presentation, expressing hope that this will be another war! Colours together. Placed in the anteroom. Remainder of the battalion was marched over to Roubaix to see the presentation. 16OR demobilized. 4 officer — 2/Lt C.P. Savage.	C
	26th		Heavy fall of snow during the night. Snow continued with the day. Church service for all concerned. Firing hard all day. 19 other ranks to be demobilized — 2/USR Bourgess.	
	27th		Gun guns lectures on travel & adventure in Egypt. Open English guard by L/Sgt S. Grenston for the winning at RONCQ. Concerning Officer presented medals to those left in for the winning teams of the Inter-Company Football & Inter-Unit War Competition. Still freezing very cold. Good wood scarce. 32OR demobilized, including the Band Sergeant.	
	28th		Normal. Still freezing. Baths as usual. 20OR demobilized.	
	29th		Normal. Still freezing. Apportion of pit lashes & filled with sufficient straw to do with all. Instructions for cleaning snow on chief roads issued by Corps. Length of road given to Battalion is 3 1/2 miles, which will be maximum amount to platoons possible being 300 men quite 12 yards to each man! As the amount of labour available decreases daily owing to demobilization. 16OR demobilized	D

WAR DIARY
or
INTELLIGENCE SUMMARY.
(Erase heading not required.)

Army Form C. 2118.

January 1919

Place	Date	Hour	Summary of Events and Information	Remarks and references to Appendices
ROUEN F.S.	29th cont		Agricultural Company disbanded & all personnel returned to this Battn. Misspelt as "Administrative Unit".	
	30th		Still pressing harder than ever. Owing to continual decrease of personnel, an order given to economize technical labour such as Signallers, Company Clerks & also H&E Amalgamations of every two platoons (Labour) & Auxiliaries combined. Decided by O.C. that the M.B. Bdr. S.I.OR & allowance of equipment should be afiliated to this Battalion. All equipment taken over to days in consequence 2/OR's alloted to take over to Tokeo 759.	E.
	31st		Normal. Very cold. Commanding Officer lectured to Battalion on First 3 months of the War. 10 Officers + NF Lieut. CAREY struck off strength of Battalion as per Studize in UK whilst on leave.	

Total numbers demobilised during the month, including those demobilised in UK:—
7 Officers 212 O.Ranks.

Numbers demobilised during Dec. 1918. 25 "

Total to date. 7 Officers. 237 O.Ranks

(Signed) M.M. Roberts Lt Col
Comdg 20th Middlesex Regt.

All Coys   P.M.C.
2/ic   R.S.M.
QM.   War Diary ✓
TO.

_____

Lorries & GS wagons

Allotment of above is as follows:-

GS wagons.

1 wagon.   Officers valises
            (QM stores. 8 johns.)

1 wagon.   QM Stores.

Lorries   15 journey

1 Lorry. A Company
1 Lorry. B Company.
1 Lorry. Canteen, Officers Mess,
                   Sgts Mess,
                   Bands Rifles Etc.

(PTO)

Lorries cont'd.

2nd Journey

   1 Lorry C Company
   1 Lorry D Company
   1 Lorry OM (extras)

Lt S W CAREY will remain for 2nd
Lorry Journey & see that everything
is moved.

                        Colin Luce
                        Capt n/Lt
2/1/19   20th Middlesex Regt

20th Battalion, Middlesex Regiment.
------oo0oo------

M O V E   O R D E R S   2-1-19.

ROUTINE FOR Jan: 3rd.

    Captain of the week:- Lieut: A.J.JOHNSON.
    Orderly Officer:- 2/Lieut: G.S.BALDWIN.
    Next for duty:- 2/Lieut: H.H.C.SMITH.
    Company for duties:- "B"
    Reveille:- 0700 hrs.
    Sick Parade:- 0715 "
    Breakfast:- 0730 "
    Guard dismounted:- 0800 hrs.

1. The Battalion will move to BONDUES Area by march route on January 3rd, 1919.

2. ORDER OF MARCH. Drums, H.Q. & "A", "B", Band, "C", "D", Transport. Head of the column will cross Rue de ROUBAIX at 0955 hrs. 100 yards between companies and 25 yards between each 6 vehicles will be maintained. Dress:- Full marching order, Jerkins to be worn under the tunic.

3. LORRIES. Allotment of Lorries will be made known as soon as possible.

4. BLANKETS AND KIT. Blankets will be rolled in 10s, securely tied and labelled and stacked by Companies by 0815 hrs. Other Company Kit will be similarly stacked by 0815 hrs.
Each man will carry his own plate, and all men in possession of library books will be responsible for carrying them.

5. OFFICERS' VALISES, will be stacked at Quartermaster's Stores by 0830 hrs.

6. MESS KIT. Officers' Mess Kit will be ready for loading at Officers' Mess by 0915 hours. Sergeants' Mess Kit will be at "A" Company Billet ready for loading by 0915 hrs.

7. DRUMS AND BAND Rifles and Equipment will be stacked at Quartermaster's Stores by 0900 hrs.

8. Billets will be left scrupulously clean. Os C. Companies will report to the Adjutant prior to moving off that they have personally inspected all billets and rooms occupied by their men.

9. Arrival in Billets in BONDUES will be notified to the Orderly Room as soon as possible.

                (sd) COLIN SHEE, Captain and Adjutant,
                    20th Battalion, Middlesex Regiment.

O.C. "A" Company,
    "B" Company,
    "C" Company,
    "D" Company.
Second in Command.
Education Officer.
Demobilization Officer.
R.S.M.
Officers' Mess.

PARADES.

Whilst in this Area parades will be held under the following arrangements:-

MONDAYS.) Parades under Company arrangements 0900 - 1200 hrs.
) for Drill, Kit Inspections, P.T. Games and Recreation,
TUESDAYS.) and any special training that may be ordered.
) Unnecessary long parades are to be avoided.
THURSDAYS.) All personnel attending the Education Classes will be
) under the Education Officer all the morning.
FRIDAYS.) The usual 2 hours out of doors will be enforced in
         the afternoon.

WEDNESDAYS.) 0900 - 1000 hrs. Full strength parades under
SATURDAYS.) Company arrangements. Inspection and P.T. Games.
) 1030 - 1200 noon. Battalion Parade, full strength.
No Education Classes will be held in the mornings.
The only exceptions to this parade will be those enumerated below:-

B.H.Q.
Officers' Mess Staff.   Demobilization Staff.
Quarter Guard.   Canteen Personnel.
"C" Company Guard.   Aid Post Personnel.
4 Signallers.   6 Runners.
Orderly Room Staff.   H.Q. Cooks.
Pioneers.   Police.
Q.M.Stores.   Sanitary Squad.
Transport.
Companies.
4 Cooks.   i Billet Orderly per Building.

BATHS. Baths at BONDUES are allotted to the Battalion on
    TUESDAYS 0830 - 1200 hrs. 1330 - 1600 hrs. and on
    FRIDAYS. 1330 - 1600 hrs.
    Allotment will be made in Battalion Routine Orders.

(sd) COLIN SHEE,
Captain and Adjutant,
20th Battn: Middlesex Regiment.

PRESENTATION OF COLOURS.

Address to the Troops by Lieutenant-General
Sir BEAUVOIR de LISLE, K.C.B., D.S.O.,
Commanding XV Corps.

In recognition of the services rendered to the Empire by your Battalion, His Majesty the King has been pleased to present you with colours, thereby placing you on the same footing as the distinguished permanent Battalions of your Regiment.

In this campaign colours have not been carried into action as was formerly the custom but I hope that in future campaigns the old custom will be resumed. In consequence there are many who do not realise all that the colours stand for. A Battalion, being composed of individuals, can cease to exist; its spirit can never die. The soul of the Battalion is represented by its colours, and to defend the honour of a Regiment, men have willingly given their lives in the past and will again in the future.

On demobilization your colours will be deposited in some place of honour, probably in the cathedral, and in the future you will perhaps conduct with pride your children and your childrens' children to see the emblem of the Battalion in which you fought in the Great War.

Should this colour, never fail to remind them of the fighting spirit of our great nation and how all right-minded men rallied at the call of duty to defend our shores from invasion and humanity from oppression.

Should this call be heard in the lives of future generations may one and all again rally to the colours of the Regiments wherever it may be necessary to unfurl them.

O.C. "A" Company,
    "B" Company,
    "C" Company,
Offr i/c H.Qrs.,
Quartermaster,
Transport Officer
M.O.
Education Officer.
Demobilization Offr.

INSTRUCTIONS FOR SNOW-CLEARING.

In the event of a heavy fall of snow the Battalion is responsible for clearing roads as under:-

LINSELLES - MOUVEAUX. From X Rds in Village to X. Roads in Village.

2. Sectors will be allotted to Companies as follows:-

"A" Company - MOUVEAUX X rds to CHIEF GLANCER X Rds (N/E.T.&)
H.Qrs & "B" Coy. CHIEF GLANCER X Rds to X Rds SE/E.W.S.&
"C" Company. - X Rds SE/E.W.S.& to LINSELLES X Rds.

3. If orders to clear snow are issued, Companies will parade as strong as possible. Only personnel as left off Ceremonial Parades are to be exempt. Education Classes will not be held and all other fatigues will be cancelled.
All Officers will parade.

4. Battalion tools will be issued, as far as possible a shovel per man. Special instructions regarding the carriage of tools will be issued if necessary.

5. A single way track 9 feet wide should be cleared first. All labour to work on the right-hand side of the road, facing North-West.

6. When the road is cleared for single way traffic, the labour should be concentrated on widening this to 18 feet.

7. When this is completed "grips" should be cut in the heap of snow on either side to allow the water to drain away when the snow melts.

8. In the village all channels and gulleys must be cleared.

9. Special Orders will be issued regarding the use of centres if required.

10. Company Commanders must be prepared to turn out every available man if necessary.

11. Special Orders will be issued regarding N.C.Os and men pending Demobilization.

Captain and Adjutant,
20th Battalion Middlesex Regiment.

29-1-19.

ROUTINE ORDERS
by
Lieut: Col: C.E.M.RICHARDS, M.C., Comdg., 20th Middlesex Reg't.
****

Part I.   Issue No: 22.   29-1-19.

Captain of the Week:- Lieut: A.J.JOHNSON.
Orderly Officer tomorrow:- Lieut: J.J.FLORETY.
Next for Duty:- 2/Lieutenant H.N.TANNER.
Company for duties:- "D"

			No: 3 Platoon.
Reveille:-	0700 hrs.	Fire Picquet:-	6 "
Breakfast:-	0800 hrs.		12 "
Sick Parade:-	0930 hrs.		15 "

1. **PARADES.**   0900 - 0945 hrs.   Amalgamation.
                  1000 - 1100 hrs.   Education.
                  1115 - 1200 hrs.   Amalgamation.

2. **AMALGAMATION.** The following amalgamations will take place tomorrow, January 30th, 1919:-
    (i) Platoons. All Companies will form two platoons per Company only. The odd numbered platoons will be retained in each case. Men will be closed up in billets under the orders of the Os C. Companies.
    (ii) Companies.
        (a) "A" & "B" Companies will be formed into one company of 4 platoons - Nos: I, III, V, and VII under the Command of Captain F.MAXWELL-LAWFORD,, for all purposes (except pay) to be known as "A" Company.
        (b) "B" Companys' Sergeant-Major and Coy: Q.M.Sergt: will retain their appointments in the composite company.
        (c) Men will be closed up in billets and the best billets selected by Captain Maxwell-Lawford.
        (d) The following items will be dealt with separately in the composite company:-
            1. Pay. Men of "B" Company must be paid on a separate Acquittance Rolls from men of "A" Company.
            2. Mobilization Stores. (if any are still in possession of companies.)
            3. Lewis Guns and Equipment (at present stored under Battalion arrangements.)
        (e) Duties. The following modifications in Battalion Duties will be brought into operation after the amalgamation:-
            1. Fire Picquet. This will consist of 3 platoons only.
            2. Duty Company. The Composite "A" Company will be Duty Company every other day.
        (f) Cooks. One Cooker only will be used by the Composite Company, and will be selected by Captain F.Maxwell-Lawford, Only cooks as required, i.e. 4, will be retained and O. C. Company will render to Orderly Room on completion of amalgamation the names of any cooks so released.
        (g) Correspondence. All correspondence for the Composite Company will be addressed to "O.C. 'A' Company".
    (iii) Completion of all amalgamations will be wired to Orderly Room.

(sd) COLIN SMEE, Captain & Adjutant,
20th Battalion Middlesex Reg't.

NOTICE.

FOOTBALL.

The Battalion Football Match against the 12th Battalion, Suffolk Regiment, fixed for tomorrow, has been postponed, indefinitely.

Vol 33

WAR DIARY.

20th Batt. Middlesex Regt.

FEBRUARY 1919.

Army Form C. 2118.

WAR DIARY
or
INTELLIGENCE SUMMARY.
(Erase heading not required.)

Instructions regarding War Diaries and Intelligence Summaries are contained in F. S. Regs., Part II. and the Staff Manual respectively. Title pages will be prepared in manuscript.

Place	Date	Hour	Summary of Events and Information	Remarks and references to Appendices

A6945 Wt.W14422/M1160 35,000 12/16 D.D.&L. Forms/C./2118/14.

WAR DIARY
INTELLIGENCE SUMMARY

Army Form C. 2118.

February 1919

Place	Date	Hour	Summary of Events and Information	Remarks and references to Appendices
Buttques	1st		Normal. Very Cold. 26 OR demobilized	
	2nd		Still very cold. C of E services only. The Rev W. Chaplain's pocket thermometer's recorded 10R demobilized 2nd Officers i/cs & Knives 9.5. 13°at 12 N. A	A
	3rd		Normal. Still Cold. The Battalion Event Party gave an entertainment which considering the tremendous difficulties under which they worked was extraordinarily good. 42 ORs demobilized.	
	4th		Normal. Owing to reduction in numbers the Quarter Guard mounted at Retreat (7.00hrs) dismounted at 9.30hrs the following morning in future. Final 5/ Battalion Interplatoon Competition played off this afternoon in the snow. No 3 v No 13 Platoon. No 13 Platoon the winners by 6 goals to nil.	
	5th		Normal. Army orders XIII & XIV of 29 January 1919 first received regarding the formation of the Armies of Occupation & Bonuses to be paid men elected to Jan 1st 1916 in spite of their ABs 64 shewing a later date. 10R demobilized who took leave to Company's billets.	B
	6th		Normal. Heavy fall of Snow last night. Amalgamation of C & D Companies. OS proved, orders carried out, moved D Company to C Company's billets owing to telephone line to Role being down, orders regarding having to go	

		Army Form C. 2118.

WAR DIARY
INTELLIGENCE SUMMARY.
(Erase heading not required.)

February 1919

Place	Date	Hour	Summary of Events and Information	Remarks and references to Appendices
BUNDLES	6.	(M)	Should sizes of the roads not received until 10:30 hrs — Consequently everything much delayed in view of numbers on parade and the case of O.+ P.Coy Amalgamation being in progress. However as many men as possible turned out 9-3 hours work by each Company finished but to ensure being served at 14:00 hrs. Great consternation caused by orders being received to hand all men had. To be divided into 3 classes — A. For demobilization — B. Those temporarily retained in the Army — C. Army of Occupation — D. Regular Army. Brigade saying that they wanted Nominal Rolls by Feb 10th. Nominal Rolls essential anyway for the battalion use, but quite unnecessary for Brigade who to-day countermanded their order + said they only wanted approximate numbers under each heading + those try to muster Feb. 7th. This if course doubtless the work of O.+ C Companies who have now to make an estimation of the numbers by to-morrow + also accurate nobelly Feb 10th/15th! Lord Derby's declared the Battalion on "The worlds Please ———— from German Domination." 41. OR Demobilized	

WAR DIARY
or
INTELLIGENCE SUMMARY.
(Erase heading not required.)

Army Form C. 2118.

February 1919

Place	Date	Hour	Summary of Events and Information	Remarks and references to Appendices
BONQUE	7th		Normal. Headquarters Transport and Battalion Transport Manoeuvres but they were paraded up — so only got a clean (?) change of clothing. 290R Demobilized. 90R sent to Junior Officers Course Aldershot as far in to instruct Readers.	
	8th		Normal. Snow shovelling in the morning. 40R Demobilized.	
	9th		Normal. C of E parades only. No other Chaplains available. Officers: F.E. ATWATER.	
			G. 240Rs Demobilized	(infantry base chap) Transport
	10th		Normal. Snow shovelling in the morning. 10 OR Demobilized. Officer attached to XI Corps Horse Shoeing & Collecting Camp for duty. This is the Middlesex Demobilizing times. O.C. BARKER despatched to England for duty with 4th Middlesex proceeding overseas. Orders received that the Battal: would proceed to provide Escorts for Rail trans proceeding to HAZEBROUCK & FIVES, many lines. On the 12th inst. 45 officers	
	11th		120 ORs moving to Hazebrouck & the remainder to FIVES on the 12:13:31 for that purpose. Orders somewhat vague. No details as to transport etc available as yet received. Preparatory orders issued. Preparations for move to-morrow. Platoons redistributed as follows:—	C.

WAR DIARY
or
INTELLIGENCE SUMMARY.
(Erase heading not required.)

Army Form C. 2118.

February 1919.

Place	Date	Hour	Summary of Events and Information	Remarks and references to Appendices
BONDUES	Feb 1st		4 platoons per Company - 2 platoons per Company from Reinforcements under A.O. XIV of 29/1/19 - 2 platoons per Company composed of the remainder, 12 men for Demobilization, men temporary returned under A.O. XIV including Battalion Cadre. Owing to no instructions being received the Battalion Cadre had been selected from reinforcements only. Detailed instructions for move of personnel to Hazebrouck, & with four men SP Battalion to FIVES 16-mmrs issued. Battalion again frozen up, only a clean change of clothing available for the Battalion. 2/Lt. RALPH DAWKINS Enlisted "E" 11/1/19. [Capt + Adjt. R. STARKING. M.E. C/FBP good, and 2/Lt. R.F. MURRAY. proceeded for Army of Occupation arrived 14.20 hrs. Remainder]	D E
	Feb 2nd		Pans. left for HAZEBROUCK at 9.30 hrs & arrived for FIVES left at 12.00 & arrived at FIVES at 3.30 pm & being held up at the Madeleine level crossing for 3/4 hour or more. All barrack stores moved to Q.M. Stores & 20 R. left to guard them. Immediately on departure from BONDUES the whole civilian population exuded from their hovels to scrounge and the evacuated billets, particularly the Q.M. Stores. On arrival at FIVES from the M.G. Battalion had left but picked up the OC & Adjutant & got what information was possible	

Army Form C. 2118.

WAR DIARY
or
INTELLIGENCE SUMMARY.
(Erase heading not required.)

February 1915

Army Form C. 2118.

Place	Date	Hour	Summary of Events and Information	Remarks and references to Appendices
FYZABAD	12	15.30	but which was not much. Great difficulty over the accommodation of the troops. Consists of a Company only with about 3 Officers instead of 12. No transport, or any Battn: equipment such as was in our possession however by dint of struggling with the Town Major - the local pundits - whether he had any recital of his responsibilities is the U.K. better arrangements were made, J.O. Room, Dunbibigats Officers & Officers billets were provided by the Officers concerned. Fires & fully little place altogether. Discovered that a Standing Guard had to be on duty at the Goods Station, that sufficient men were present down each day to Ayodhyr to make up postage sent. Pack Trans. also discovered that the personnel sent down had to march to STANORE Stati.	
	13		to catch the 6.0 p.m passenger Train each day. Some 1½ hours march. All available personnel utilised on clearing billets. Arrangements made for a totidi guard turnout outside the Battal: Killer (Winston Sper Retreat to Reveille. - to equip the standi guard with 20 rounds S.A.A. per man & to provide Signallers at the Town Major's Office - this letter giving	

WAR DIARY
INTELLIGENCE SUMMARY.
(Erase heading not required.)

Army Form C. 2118.

February 1915

Place	Date	Hour	Summary of Events and Information	Remarks and references to Appendices
FIVES	13th		# Communicated through Army to W Corps to W Division to Brigade, with truth, and also, with truth, through Army to IGC to IAmy to Corps to the Town Major at Hazebrouck, that 50 to OC Detachment; through Army would go Through by this means it was never possible to speak 4 escorts arrived from Hazebrouck + 1 escort + Monsoon it being discovered that trains went to Muscron + some to HK possibly some to other places. quickly knew where they would get to until they arrived. 14 OR sent down to Hazebrouck, + discovered that all probability there would be a shortage + none at Hazebrouck before very long. 14 OR Demobilized	
	14th		Continued clearing up + proceed to Billets. 3 escorts arrived for Hazebrouck but unknown how this elsewhere. the question of reducing numbers of men at FIVES gone into very carefully, a will demobilizate still continuing urgent representation made that it be had not sufficient men to provide escorts for the number of trains going through to Hazebrouck. 34 OR returned to Hazebrouck. 4 OR demobilized	
	15th		Notice. 3 Escorts received for Hazebrouck ← 54 OR sent down. be detachment rapid. Ma 1146 OR sent off in 48 hours = 19 Escorts, of which only 9 received at FIVES !!	

WAR DIARY
INTELLIGENCE SUMMARY.
(Erase heading not required.)

Army Form C. 2118.

February 1919

Place	Date	Hour	Summary of Events and Information	Remarks and references to Appendices
FIVES	15th Feb		Definite arrangements drawn up for feeding, accommodation, & dealing with Train Escorts arriving from Hazebrouck. Absorbik a view to increasing personnel available for Escorts, all personnel employed at FIVES Sidings to a minimum. Consequently jobs & workings were beginning to settle down.	F
		At 11.45 am	Orders received (consists of about 4 lines of Telegraphic type) that the Battalion would move to ST ANDRÉ tomorrow 16th Sunday.	G
			What a shock. It was possible to send out orders issued. 40R demobilized including 2nd OR Clerks.	
	16th		Orders for move issued first thing in the morning - Stores moved by MT during the mornings owing to thaw precautions. No lorries could be obtained but 5 cars & 98 wagons materially hindered turned up & assisted, owing to a number of Horses having been demobilized only a few of these transport could be moved. ie 1 Cooker, 1 Water Cart, 1 Mess Cart, 1 Mule Cart. Remainder afterday. 2 or more journeys, left of sent back to put up at FIVES for the night. Static guard had to be left & also all Musketeers Shoes with a guard over this. At 14.00hrs the remainder of the personnel consisting of some 12 Officers & 14 men marched off, in slight rain, which slowly increased to a steady downpour. Arriving in the Square at TULLE met the T.O. who reported to be	H

WAR DIARY
or
INTELLIGENCE SUMMARY.
(Erase heading not required.)

Army Form C. 2118.

February 1919

Place	Date	Hour	Summary of Events and Information	Remarks and references to Appendices
FIVES / ST ANDRÉ	16th cont.		at least 2 Motor detachments of personnel for Tran. Escorts were at nights to get the artillies. On view of the fact that the C.O., Staff Capt. & Billeting Officer had already been over to arrange selected billets in conjunction with the Havana Commandant this promised a fairly hectic time ahead. Having got 2/3rds of the way out by a guide who informed us that we had motored out of our billets & that he was to guide us to the new ones. It turned out that these billets were at le CANON D'OR, some 20mm. where were away from the Officers billets, H.Q. Mess, Orderly Room & soon. At 4:30 pm arrived at le Canon D'OR & billeted the men in two large empty chateaux [apparently of exterior with not a stick of barrack furniture. However all personnel accommodated by 6 pm. Of 12-15- transferring the Q.M. stores from the original dump to a push billet the move completed with this except of stores left at FIVES & transport lines by 7:30 pm. 3 Escorts arrived but none sent down to Hazebrouck. In spite of it all 7 O.R. demobilized. Officer 10/M Transfer Jones demobilized at Wilson Cleave to K. 9/1/19	

WAR DIARY
INTELLIGENCE SUMMARY.
(Erase heading not required.)

February 1919

Army Form C. 2118.

Place	Date	Hour	Summary of Events and Information	Remarks and references to Appendices
St ANDRÉ	17th		Organisation of means for receipt of War Escorts from Hazebrouck. Labour accommodation & personnel of the necessarily retained at St André is being St Cann GOR. 10ffr and 30 OR from 15 I F N.Lancs attached to the Battn. No original personnel available for War Escorts Guard at F./E.S./ St A still has to tr 5 War Escorts, though officially supposed to be divided. St André, not allowed to get off the trains unless properly relieved. 8 Escorts arrived from Hazebrouck & 27 OR sent down. 40R demobilised	
	18th		Normal. 4 Escorts received, 58 OR sent down. Wires received re "Brigade" Armistice Growth, has been prolonged. Cpl on detached personnel returned to the Battn. Assumption by the name by a certain Sergeant at last officially announced after original application being submitted in December 1916 !!! Capt 9H SCRIVEN returned to O.G.	
	19th		Normal. 3 Escorts received & 56 OR returned. Releasable personnel at XI Corps H.Staff's Cup returned to/C personnel. All strands of 10ffr, HOR for American A.P.M.'s received.	
	20th		Normal. 9 Escorts received & 38 ORs despatched. 10ffr A/Lt D. APPLEBY demobilised. Whilst on leave to U.K.	

WAR DIARY
or
INTELLIGENCE SUMMARY

Army Form C. 2118.

February 1919

Place	Date	Hour	Summary of Events and Information	Remarks and references to Appendices
STANDRIE	21st		Normal. 3 escorts received & 49 ORs despatched, in ones of President POINCARÉ arriving at Hazebrouck organising a guard of honour — His approval selected by R.T.O. Hazebrouck!	
	22nd		Countryside searched for Bolshs. Only available place — The Municipal Baths, like where no clean clothes available. Arranged with Bde to draw 300 sets of clothing. 6 escorts received & 42 ORs despatched.	{Church parade washed out in favour of Baths.}
	23rd		Normal. 4 escorts received & 29 ORs despatched. Arrangements for Baths Hot-rooms & issue of clean clothing from Ord.Store's previous Baths issued. 20 OR demobilized. Walsh's case originally struck off Strength as deserter! Discovered to be Pak'nd working on shortage of coal. Baths utilised at plast!	
	24th		5 escorts received & 51 OR despatched. Recruiting Campaign opened — the battalion. Information with regard to despatch of personnel received contingent with to lift all arms.	
	25th		Normal. 5 escorts arrived. 92 OR despatched. Informat' received thro' the Postal Cadre is to be considered as part of Machinery of Demobilization, as such is entitled to full bonus from 1/2/19. Capt. g. Kerwen appointed Armorer as re 5/2/19	{2/Lt P.O.H.E.S Instructions for A/TO.}
	26th		Normal. 2 escorts received & no men despatched to Hazebrouck. Orders received.	

Army Form C. 2118.

WAR DIARY
or
INTELLIGENCE SUMMARY.
(Erase heading not required.)

February 1919.

Place	Date	Hour	Summary of Events and Information	Remarks and references to Appendices
St ANDRÉ	26th	Cal.b	Met some detachments from various battalions & divisions will be sent to reinforce us then. — 80 wills, 60 from 36th Divs & 60 from 40th Divs. What will arranged for sufficient personnel to relieve those at Hazebrouck, provide for lorries to St ANDRÉ, men from Hazebrouck camps to St ANDRÉ, m.t. for M.T. parties for day after arrival. Army of Occupation men being sent to 1st Middlesex. Hoare, on 2/3/19 & L.N. Lanes detachments returned to their battln on employ relief. In lieu it will be pers. such if no "entrainment" occurs. 2/ow began return for ASFC. Result of Recruiting Campaign so far is 4 NCOs & 12 enlistments (Total 9-25) 2 volunteers for 1 year with the army of occupation, 1 volunteer for 2 years service as a clerk with the A.P.C. if transfer approved. 10 R.M.R. Details/offices received BWR.	
	27th		60 wills arrived at 11.00 hrs. 60 men from 26th Divisn, 30 from 13th Battn + 30 from 9th Battn R.I.F. arrived at Hazebrouck by train, instead of lorries to with the rations. 60 men from 40th Division arrived at Hazebrouck at 5:30pm about 9:30pm. Middlesex personnel from Hazebrouck arrives St ANDRÉ + Loires. Middlesex thus all Middlesex men collected at St ANDRÉ.	

Army Form C. 2118.

WAR DIARY
or
INTELLIGENCE SUMMARY.
(Erase heading not required.)

February 1919

Place	Date	Hour	Summary of Events and Information	Remarks and references to Appendices
ST ANDRÉ	27/2/19		Preparation for despatching Army of Occupation men carried on, & order re cleaning up issued. Essentes received but no sundown.	I
	28/2		The last day of our demob holds. 4 O.R.s demobilized. Men appear anxious to desire to regular for 2 years but unfortunately no papers in possession for the time being.	
			6 Officers & 226 O.R demobilized during the month. 26 Horses & 2 mules demobilized during the month.	

Myself Roberts Lt Colonel
Cmdg 20th Middlesex Regt

28/2/19

N O T I C E.

20th Middlesex Regiment.
CONCERT PARTY.

"T H E   S C R O U N G E R S"

in a Drop of

BLACK and WHITE.

***

including

The Farcial Sketch, entitled -

"SHEAROFF HOME, the 'SAFE' MAN".

****

Entirely New Songs, Scenery, Dresses, etc.

****

Monday 3rd February, 1919, in the Black Hut in rear
of "C" Company's Billet.

Doors Open 1730 hrs.   Commence 1800 hrs Sharp.

****

ADMISSION - FREE.

"THE SCROUNGERS"
in a Drop of
BLACK and WHITE.

PROGRAMME.

1st Tot.	Opening Chorus.		The Troupe.
2nd Tot.	Song.	"Shipmates O' Mine"	Sig Brightwell.
3rd Tot.	Concerted Item.	"Eight Little Motorists"	The Troupe.
4th Tot.	Humorous Song.	"Blue Italian Band"	C.S.M. J.Miller.
5th Tot.	Song.	"One of the B'hoys"	2/Lt: P.Benda.
6th Tot.	Specialty Act.	Conjuring.	Pte H.Glick.
7th Tot.	Song.	"Ragging the Raggedy Doo"	Pte E.J.McPherson.
8th Tot.	Song.	"For You Alone"	Pte F.Duckett.
9th Tot. (A Double)	Humorous Interlude	" ? "	Those Two Again.
10th Tot.	Song.	"Moonlight"	Sig Brightwell.
11th Tot.	Trio.	"The Huntsmen"	2/Lt Benda. Pte Duckett. C.S.M. Miller.
12th Tot.	A Closing Chorus in Disguise.	"Hush-a-bye Baby".	The Troupe.

Interval.

Farcial Sketch, entitled

"SHEAROFF HOME, THE 'SAFE' MAN"

in Two Scenes.

CAST.

SHEAROFF HOME.	Dvr R.HOUSTON.
FLASHINGTON FOBBS.	2/Lt P.BENDA.
JEREMIAH JERKIN.	C.S.M. J.MILLER.
WILLIAM BUNG.	Pte E.J.McPHERSON.
CLARISSA BUNG.	Cpl E.W.HARRIS.
JENKINS - The Waiter.	Pte H.GLICK.
Dr WATSON.	Pte F.DUCKETT.

Scene 1. Exterior of Country Inn.   Scene 11. Interior of Inn.

THE KING

At the Piano - Corporal E.W.HARRIS.
Scenic Artiste - Corporal J.JOHNSON.

3. AMALGAMATION. (i) "C" and "D" Companies will be amalgamated to one Company of 4 platoons (Nos: 8, 11, 13 & 15.) on Thursday Feb: 6th, 1919, under arrangements to be made between the present Company Commanders concerned.
(ii) The Composite Company will be known as "D" Company and will be accommodated in "C" Company's Billet.
(iii) The Composite Company will be under the Command of 2/Lieut: F.BENDA.
(iv) The following items will be dealt with separately in the Composite Company:-
    1. Pay. Men of "C" Company must be paid on separate Acquittance Rolls from men of "D" Company.
    2. Mobilization Stores (if there are any still in possession of Companies.
    3. Lewis Guns and equipment (at present stored under Battalion arrangements.
(v) The following modifications in Battalion Duties will be brought into operation after the amalgamation, commencing Friday February 7th:-
    (a) Duty Company. "A" & "D" Companies will be duty company on alternate days.
    (b) Fire Picquet. This will consist of 2 platoons only. These platoons will after the amalgamation, commencing on Friday Feb: 7th, parade at their own Company Lines at Roll Call and will be reported present, or otherwise, to the Orderly Officer by the Coy: Orderly N.C.O., concerned.

(Continued)

3. AMALGAMATIC. (Continued).
    (vi) Cooks. One Cooker only will be used by the Composite Company and will be selected by 2/Lieutenant P.BRICK. Only Cooks as required, i.e. 4, will be retained and O.C. Company will render to Orderly Room on completion of amalgamation the names of any cooks so released.
    (vii) Correspondence. All correspondence for the Composite Company will be addressed to the O.C. "D" Company.
    (viii) Completion of amalgamation will be wired to the Orderly Room.

20TH BATTALION MIDDLESEX REGIMENT

MOVE ORDER NO.1.   10.2.1919.

1. The following moves will take place on February 12th:-

    (a) 4 Officers and 120 O.Rs. will move by Lorry to HAZEBROUCK to relieve 104th M.G. Company guarding trains.

    (b) The Battalion, less the Railway Guard (see above) will move by march route to FIVES near LILLE.

2. **Reference 1.(a) above.**

    This guard will be constituted as follows:-

    Captain F. MAXWELL-LAWFORD.   In Command.

    Lieut. J.J. ASHWORTH. M.M.)
    2.Lieut. E.L. WILLMOTT M.C.)   "D" Company.

    2.Lieut. V.W.M. NUNN.   "A" Company.

    Each Company will find one platoon of not less than 60 men with a proportion of N.C.Os., from the personnel noted for the Army of Occupation under A.O.XIV. If sufficient senior N.C.Os are not available from this personnel, they must be taken from those available for release, or temporarily retained under A.O.XIV. Being on this duty will in no way affect the release of a N.C.O. available for demobilization.

    Nominal rolls of personnel selected will be rendered to Orderly Room as soon as the party is despatched.

    Further details will be issued when received.

    Lieut. J.J. FLOREY will take over Command of "A" Coy. during the temporary absence of Captain F. MAXWELL-LAWFORD.

3. **Reference 1.(b) above.**

    Full details of this move will be issued when received.

Copies to:- O.C. "A" Company.   Medical Officer.
           O.C. "D"   "   Transport Officer.
           Quartermaster.   P.M.C.
           Demobilization Officer.   Adjutant.
           Education Officer.   War Diary.
           A/C.O.M.S.M.O.

                                    Captain and Adjutant,
                                    20th Battalion Middlesex Regiment.

10.2.1919.

20TH BATTALION MIDDLESEX REGIMENT

MOVE ORDER NO. 2.   11.2.1919.

Detailed instructions for move of your personnel are as follows:-

1. Total strength of party will be 150 all ranks.

2. 6 Lorries will report at 08.00 hours on 12th inst. at these Headquarters. Your party my will parade at these Headquarters with full equipment and blankets etc. at that time.

3. Advance party will be sent as already instructed.

4. Rations for consumption 13th. inst. will be taken. Rations for consumption 14th inst. and onwards will be drawn from R.S.O. HAZEBROUCK.

5. A copy of XV Corps Orders for preventing Looting of Supply Trains is attached, in as much as it effects your Company.

6. The Commanding Officer remains in Command of the whole Battalion.   You will be in communication by telephone with Battn. H.Q. at FIVES.   Arrange to have 2 Signallers in your party.

7. As far as can be ascertained the escorts provided by you must bring full equipment each time they escort a supply train, as similar numbers are sent down to you daily from the Battalion by passenger train, and the escorts remain with the Battalion at the completion of the journey.

8. All local orders for guards, checkers, etc. will be handed over on relief.

9. Additional duties required by the R.T.O's concerned will be notified and arranged direct with Officers Commanding at FIVES and HAZEBROUCK.   The latter is presumably yourself.

10. The accomodation at HAZEBROUCK is very poor, but there is a Cinema.

11. Completion of relief will be wired to Battn. H.Q.

Captain & Adjutant,
20th Battn. Middlesex Regiment.

Copies to:-

Capt. F. MAXWELL-LAWFORD.

O.C. "D" COMPANY.

QUARTERMASTER.

ADJUTANT.

WAR DIARY. ✓

20TH BATTALION MIDDLESEX REGIMENT

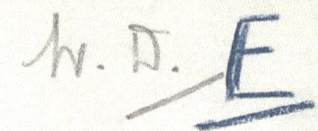

MOVE ORDER NO. 3.   11.2.1919.

1. Detailed instructions for the move of the Battalion to FIVES as follows:-

2. LORRIES. 5 lorries will be available and will be allotted as follows. 2.Lieut. A.E.C.SMITH will be responsible for their distribution.
   (a) "A" Company.   1. To carry Company blankets, Coy Officers' valises, Company Stores etc.
   (b) "D" Company.   1. To carry Company blankets, Coy Officers' valises, Company Stores, band instruments, and Concert party stores.
   (c) Headquarters.   1. To carry H.Q. blankets, H.Q.Officers' valises Orderly Room Stores, Demobilization Stores, Officers' Mess kit.
   (d) Quartermaster. 2. One to go to Q.M.Stores direct. One to go to H.Q., pick up L.Gun Stores under direction of L.G.Officer, and then go on to the Q.M.Stores.
   If possible, mens' packs will be put on the lorries by Companies and Headquarters.

3. 1st Line Transport. Arrangements for horsing vehicles will be made direct with T.O. Empty limbers will be utilised by the Quartermaster by direct arrangement with the T.O.
   One limber will be detailed by T.O. to collect Canteen Stores, Education Office Stores, and Sergeants' Mess Kit, during the morning. The Maltese Cart will be sent to the Aid Post.

4. BAGGAGE Valises, blankets and packs will be stacked by Companies and Headquarters at Companies lines and Bn. H.Q. by 09.30, hrs. ready for loading.

5. Loading Parties. Os.C.Companies and H.Q. will arrange their own loading parties. Loading party for lorry shown in para II,d, collecting L.Gun Stores, will consist of six men detailed by O.C. "D" Company, to report to L.G.Officer at Bn. H.Q. at 09.00, hrs. Having loaded L.Gun Stores, this party will proceed with the lorry to Q.M.Stores and act as loading party under the direction of the Quartermaster.

6. BARRACK STORES. All Barrack Stores will be taken to Q.M.Stores by Companies, Headquarters, and all isolated sections at 09.00, hrs tomorrow. Lieut.E.P.DURAN will report to Q.M.Stores at this time and supervise the storing of these stores, which consist of Paillasses, Beds, Ablution Benches (unless fixed), forms, tables, Stoves and piping, Lanterns and lamps (if any). These will be handed over to representative of Bondues Area Commandant. Latrine buckets will be left empty.

8. RATIONS, for consumption on 13th, will be delivered to Battalion by Divisional Train during the morning. Rations for 14th instant will be drawn from R.S.O.FIVES.

9. ROUTINE for Feb,12th will be as follows:-
   Captain of the Week,   2.Lieut.P.BEEDA.M.C.
   Orderly Officer,   2.Lieut.A.E.C.SMITH.
   Next for Duty,   2.Lieut.H.FEATHER,   Duty Company.   "A"
   Reveille, 06.45, hrs. Breakfast, 07.30. Sick Parade. 09.00, hrs.
   Dinners 11.00. hrs.   Companies and H.Q. will parade on the
   LILLE ROAD in fours facing South at 12.00, hours.
   Quarter Guard will dismount at Reveille.

                                    (Sd) COLIN S.M. Captain and Adjutant,
                                         20th Battalion Middlesex Regiment.

STANDING ORDERS
for
TRAIN GUARDS ARRIVING FROM HAZEBROUCK.

****

1. N.C.O. reports to Adjutant and also R.S.M. Nutty. If arriving in the early hours of the morning, leaves a list of his party in Company Office on large table.

2. The Sergeant of the Guard has instructions as to which rooms are available as billets. N.C.O. in charge party will billet men accordingly.

3. A hot meal is always ready on the cooker. The Sergeant of the Guard will issue this to all men arriving during the early hours of the morning.

4. The N.C.O. in charge of party will ensure that his party has accommodation and are comfortable, before retiring himself.

5. 12 hours after arrival at IVES, every man from HAZEBROUCK must be properly shaved, cleaned and kit stacked neatly against the wall ready to depart when necessary, and is available for duty after this period of rest.

6. All men arriving before 22.00 hours are due to proceed to HAZEBROUCK by passenger train next day, parading at 16.00 hours. Men are therefore warned that they must not be absent from billets after 15.00 hours.

15th February, 1919.

Captain and Adjutant,
20th Battalion Middlesex Regiment.

ADMINISTRATION STAFF.

The following only are to be considered as unavailable for duty as Railway Guards, etc., and any appointments held by other personnel up to the present are to be considered cancelled.

SIGNALLERS. (7) Cpl Bishop, L/C Hunt, L/C Sainsbury, L/C Hyde, Ptes Brown, Creed, Bierman.

Bn. Runners. (4) L/C Simmer, Pte Nicholson, Pte Williams, Pte Garstang.

M.GUN. (3) Sergt. Bosies, Pte Longabeer, Pte Welford.

Lewis Gun. (2) L/C Perrin, Pte Canning.

S.O.MEN. (6) Cpl Adams, Pte Klaymaker, Pte Scott, Pte Howell, Pte Gaskell, Pte Robinson.

MEDICAL ORDERLY. (1) Pte Hohen.

Company Cooks. (5) L/C Berridge, Pte Rumsford, Pte Jayman, Pte Cole, Pte Wilson.

Sergts Mess. (2) Pte Payne, Pte Waverley.

Post Corpl. (1) L/C Lynden.

M.O.Staff. (5) Cpl Odell, Pte Gain, Pte Taylor, Pte Stotter, Pte Hill.

Pioneers. (2) Pte Blundon, Pte Owen.

Tailors. (2) Sgt. Powell, Pte Blonch.

Shoemakers. (2) Sgt. Wesson, Pte Biggle.

Coy Runners. (2) One per Company from B.H.Q. { "A" Pte Jones.
                                                  { "B" Pte Plowman.

Barbers. (1) Pte Gray.

Sanitary. (3) L/C Galsworthy, Pte Mosmoud, Pte Alexander.

Police. (1) L/C F.H.Davis.

Companies. O.M.S. "B" Coy. – Sgt. Richardson.
A/C.M.S. "A" Coy. – L/C Day.
"D" Coy. – Sgt. Gransdon.
Clerks. – One per Company.
Storemen – One per Company.
A/R.S.M. – C.S.M. O.F.Lutty.
A/O.M.S.(H) – Sgt. Holman.
Canteen. – Pte Stratford.

Officer's Servants. It has become essential to allow servants on the authorised scale only. This is one per 2 Subaltern Officers (except Company Commanders) and must be carried out forthwith as arranged with O.C. Companies.

15th February, 1919.
Captain and Adjutant,
20th Battalion Middlesex Regiment.

20th Battalion Middlesex Regiment.

MOVE ORDERS.

16/2/19.

1. The Battalion, less the HAZEBROUCK party will move to ST AMIENS to-day, 16th February, and will parade outside the Battalion Billet at 14.00 hours, facing North West.

2. Officer's Valises will be taken to the Quartermaster Stores by 11.00 hours.

3. Transport. All available vehicles will report to the Q.M.Stores at 11.00 hours to make first journey.

4. Officer's Billets. All Officers will hand into Orderly Room or T/Lieutenant ROBINSON, the number, name of street, and owner of billets occupied by them.

5. Packs will be worn.

Captain and Adjutant,
20th Battalion Middlesex Regiment.

Copies to:-

O.C. "A" Company.
      "B" Company.
R.S.M.
Transport Officer.
Quartermaster.
Officer's Mess.
Adjutant.
War Diary.

Officer Commanding,
  'A' Company.
  'D'   "
Transport Officer.
Quartermaster.
A/R.S.M.

      To-morrow, 28th inst., and following day, 1st March, are to be spent in cleaning and smartening up men who leave for the Army of Occupation on March 2nd.

      Particular points requiring attention are:-

1. BATHS. All men who have missed bathing recently to be given clean Clothes and bathed under Company arrangements.
2. Cleaning of Equipment and arms.
3. Haircutting.
4. Sewing on of buttons and minor tailoring repairs.
5. Boots.
6. Kit inspections.
7. Discipline.

      The Commanding Officer will see all the men on March 1st at 11.00 hours, at the back of "A" Company's Chateau, and B.O.C. at same place at about 17.00 hours same date.

27-2-1919.

(Signed) COLIN SMEE, Captain and Adjutant,
20th Battalion (D.C.O.) The Middlesex Regiment.

WAR DIARY

20th Batt⁄ Middlesex Reg⁄t.

MARCH 1919.

Army Form C. 2118.

WAR DIARY
or
INTELLIGENCE SUMMARY.

(*Erase heading not required.*)

Instructions regarding War Diaries and Intelligence Summaries are contained in F. S. Regs., Part II. and the Staff Manual respectively. Title pages will be prepared in manuscript.

Place	Date	Hour	Summary of Events and Information	Remarks and references to Appendices

WAR DIARY
INTELLIGENCE SUMMARY

Army Form C. 2118.

MARCH 1919

Place	Date	Hour	Summary of Events and Information	Remarks and references to Appendices
STANDRE LILLE	1st		Preparations for despatch of Army of Occupation draft completed. Farewell speeches by O.C. Brigade at 11.00 hrs to the Canadrig Officer at 17.30 hrs. Men quite happy enough drunk. Orders issued with regard to the more automatic recruits. War	A
	2nd		lorries (number unstated) would report some time to-night. Lorries arrived at about 8.30 p.m. B. of . . Detachment of 6th Wilts collected at ST ANDRE 3 Escorts camped at ranks 8.25 ors as follows P.P. PRICE Army of Occupation draft for 1st Bn Middlesex, P.P. BURMAN, T. GILES, 9 165 OR's left by lorries at 5.30 am for TOURCOING to entrain in the daily personnel train there at 6.45 am, lorries coming back to ST Audis at about 8.00 am. Administration Superb! I was picked up at Hazebrouck, making total draft 20 Officers & 166 OR's. Detachment of Wilts left by lorry at 13.00 hrs. Detachment from 4th Bde sent to relieve them by 12 noon, discovered at 5 a.m. stats at 100 hrs having been there 13 hours having no rations, were relieving a Guard of Wilts which status more/severe being made to this battalion. Personnel of W. N. Lewis collected at ST ANDRE 3 Escorts arrived from Hazebrouck our men despatched.	

Army Form C. 2118.

WAR DIARY
or
INTELLIGENCE SUMMARY.
(Erase heading not required.)

MARCH 7, 1919.

Place	Date	Hour	Summary of Events and Information	Remarks and references to Appendices
STAND HILLS	3rd		Attachment of 141 leaves. Pioneers left for their own unit at 13.00hrs. 5 escorts arrived & 50 ORs despatched to Hazebrouck.	
	4th		8 ORs demobilized. Notes of importance. In spite of this Battalion being reduced to an effective strength of 130 ORs, Orderly Room work shows no appreciable decrease. Batts. at fille for all personnel at strands. Remaining 2 companies (A&D) amalgamated into one under Capt. PRETNDA & closed up into 1 chateau. Middlesex personnel from Hazebrouck collected & authorised to provide static guards at First & Battn. Stand Guard. 6 escorts arrived from Hazebrouck & 40 ORs despatched. Batts at fille from 10.30 - 12 noon.	
	5th		Normal. 11 their escorts arrived from, & 34 ORs despatched to Hazebrouck.	
	6th		Normal. Troops payed. 4 escorts received & 69 ORs despatched.	
	7th		Normal. 10 escorts received & 6 ORs despatched. Capt. W. G. Troffe PTER demobilized army strike! 1 Sgt & 7 ORs allotted for cadre at 3½ thus, total originally having fulfilled their role & duties, 35 for bons detachment relieved by	
	8th		Normal. 3 escorts received & 10 ff 79 ORs despatched.	
			13th York Lanes	
	9th		R.C. Services only. 6 escorts received & nothing sent down. 29 ORs & 10 Officer (Capt T.W. PRUST) demobilized.	

WAR DIARY or INTELLIGENCE SUMMARY

Army Form C. 2118.

MARCH 1919

Place	Date	Hour	Summary of Events and Information	Remarks and references to Appendices
Staudré Lille	10		Normal. 3 escorts arrived & one man despatched. Detachment at Hazebrouck moved to Bailleul, where a few huts had been built for accommodation. At XV Corps provided Rat barrack furniture, should the Section get working. 4 personal escort to Bailleul to receive it, did not arrive, but it did not arrive. IOR demobilized from Divisional HQ. Canadian found on a train with loaded revolver, arrested the detective 15 April. Army or Lille holding. Batt a Lille from 10.30 a.m. to 12 noon. Clearcloths issued prior to talking.	
	11		Normal. 2 escorts received & 28 ORs despatched. 1 Escort suspended with at assaulting by a Labour Corps Officer. Doubtful solved. Major Scriven sent down to Bailleul to relieve Capt Lawford, who was required as assistant adjutant.	
	12		Snowstorm in the night, making everything very cold. 3 escorts arrived & 1 man sent down. 1 escort arriving at Orchies on 10 inst. discovered that several trucks had been broken into & traced several thousand cigarettes & 5 cases of whiskey to ROD train crew, who had the articles in their truck. Later the guess his negligence on the part of the Escort was raised by the 1st Army. It is noted of the fact that the Train arrived at Bailleul without any escort, considered the slightly amusing. IOR demobilized from Divisional HQ	
	13		Very cold. 6 escorts received & 47 ORs returning to Bailleul. State guard at FIVES moved to STANDIS, as ratin dump moved. This simplifies firing of guards.	

WAR DIARY
or
INTELLIGENCE SUMMARY.

Army Form C. 2118.

March 1919.

Place	Date	Hour	Summary of Events and Information	Remarks and references to Appendices
S! André	14th		Normal. 7 escorts arrived. + 25 O.R's despatched to Bailleul.	
file.	15th		Bulk of 76th Wurts, at Wambrechies utilized behind 9 O.R's + 13 O.R's 5 escorts received, & women sent to Bailleul in view of Batt. fwish festival (Purim) held at NIENE to-day - to-morrow. 16th inst. Guard over ratin dump at S! André stationed during the night by soldiers & civilians, armed with revolvers. Exchange of shots turned up all round, but no damage done & the dump intact at day break. Unfortunately no although forwarded, all though several officers rushed round to the station in mufti chase, + it being their last hope.	
	16th		R.C Services. None Ihr available. 3 Sscoots received + 79 O.R's despatched. Particulars of officers available for demob. Re-gaz'n, indicated to 37 years's service & those who re-for service in 1914. This excludes some 4 or 5 officers leave to twice opened, but no application as it is reported that leave is flooded at this time of year. Following extracts from gazette received:— March 12th 1919. Capt. (A/Major) C.F.M. RICHARDS. M.C. (East Lancs Regt) to Command 20th Bn Middlesex Rgt + 4th Bn Temp Lt/col. Dec 5th 1918. Seniority Sept 12th 1917. Upon appointment approved by F.M. C-in-C. Lt/H.A. HEADEN. (R.Munster Fus.) to be A/Capt whilst Commdg a Company. 24/1/25, 1st Oct 1918. T/2Lt P.BENDA. M.M. (Middlesex Rt) to be A/Capt whilst Commdg a Company. 12/11/18.	

WAR DIARY or INTELLIGENCE SUMMARY

Army Form C. 2118.

March 1919

Place	Date	Hour	Summary of Events and Information	Remarks and references to Appendices
St André Lille	17th		All S.A.A., T.M. shells & Revolver Ammunition returned to Army Ammunition dump at MENIN., less 5 boxes required to equip personnel of Cadre with 120 rds S.A.A., 3 Boxes for 10th S.H.I. & 2 Boxes for 43rd Bde H.Q. Under orders from 14th Divn. Things definitely laid down in D.R.Os that this was necessary & things were definitely laid down in Ammt. Regs. that no S.A.A. or explosives were to be taken by Cadres to Engd. This further appears to be preparation for the next war. 8 escorts arrived & 25 O.R's returned to Bailleul.	
	18th		Normal. 3 escorts received & 40 O.R's sent to Bailleul.	
	19th		Normal. 2 escorts received & 28 O.R's sent down. Extract from Gazette 18/3/19 received:- Infantry. Middlesex Regt. Lieutenant Colonel /t Ch. Montague (Retd.) Regular Forces.	
	20th		Brigadier General. PEREIRA. C.B. C.M.G. D.S.O. (Comdg 43rd Brigade) came to say farewell to all available officers & O.R's of the Battalion. 4 escorts received & 19 O.R's despatched.	
	21st		No escorts received but 16 O.R's sent down. 20 O.R's transferred to Cadre of 43rd Brigade H.Q. 6 O.R transferred to Cadre No 17 H.I. Orders received for transfer of 15 O.R to be transferred to Cadres of Battalions in 41st Brigade. 3 to 29th D.L.I., 4 to 12 to 33rd London. The Battalion thus Cadres & Battalion 3 to 29th Brigade, 3 to 29th D.L.I., 4 to 12 to 33rd London as a whole, as was the above being made to use it, to get 4 Battalions & 1 Battn H.Q. or 5 as a whole to 12th Sn Hotk. R.f. But 3 O.R have to be transferred to 12th Sn Hotk. R.f. on this occasion! Of course we were equal to this occasion!	

WAR DIARY or INTELLIGENCE SUMMARY

Army Form C. 2118.

March 1919

Place	Date	Hour	Summary of Events and Information	Remarks and references to Appendices
St André Lille	22nd		Personnel of 1st & 9th Bns R.I.F. returned to their own Division - 36th. Escorts received of 240 R Sentown. All demobilization leave stopped in view of Strikes at home. Strikes threatened at home. 8 O.R. sent to 15th Batt. Middlesex Regt. 2 officers, Lt. Col. P. Williams M.C., & 2/Lt. F. Lucas, sent for demobilization. 3 escorts received & 18 O.R's sent to Bailleul.	
	23rd		All Lewis guns & Rifles inspected by an Ordnance Wallah. Escorts received & 24 O.R's sent to Bailleul. One, Pte Jagger, returned from Wilton Prison, but died in May 1918.	
	24th		Brigade & Divisional Headquarters closed down. Correspondence carried on through all 43rd Brigade group of Cadres. Hut shortly will be this Battali. Lorries to either, is done through 15th H.L.I. Wire from H.Q.S. 14th Divisn received at 10:20 hrs ordering demobilization of the remaining 4 Officers of this Battali, to be at Place Thiers by 11:30 hrs. Horses despatched immediately but grease n.s.fi time for rehearsing inspection as stated. 2 mules loaned for the purpose of drawing returns from the D.A.C. 2 Transports received & 31 O.R's returned to Bailleul.	

Army Form C. 2118.

WAR DIARY
or
INTELLIGENCE SUMMARY.
(Erase heading not required.)

March 1919.

Place	Date	Hour	Summary of Events and Information	Remarks and references to Appendices
St André Lille	25th		Normal. 3 escorts received & 8 O.Rs sent to Bailleul. Detachment of one Officer & an escort from S. Omer to Bailleul (of XIX Corps) withdrawn to Bailleul. Trains therefore arriving unescorted at Bailleul. Officers allowed to be demobilized who are over 35 years stage or who joined in 1914 or 1915. This lets out another 4 or 5 Officers but nobody seems anxious to go. A.D.R's very terse about the orders sent away yesterday – nothing in time for retaining examination – demanding explanations. Told him to refer him directly.	
	26th		Normal. 15 escort only received & 13 O.R's sent down. Major Scriven reports that trains are now arriving at Bailleul from the Base with escorts on, detailed to remain on the train until it reached destination. Also many trains do not stop at all at Bailleul.	
	27th		A.D.R. Division Batts at Wambrechies allotted between 12 & 13 cohs. Personnel of 12th & 15th R/F 9/13 Enniskilling Fusiliers returned to their own division. 15th but not relieved. 1 Escort arrived & 10 O.R's sent down to Bailleul.	Personnel of 12th/15th R/F & 2/4 H.H.
	28th		Normal. 1 Escort arrived & 24 O.R's sent down. 2 Officers, 2/Lt Wilkes St MC & 2/Lt H.H. Tanner, & 10 O.R's demobilized thus leaving only 10 R, pending final approval of results/unit, became available for demobilisation.	

Army Form C. 2118.

WAR DIARY
or
INTELLIGENCE SUMMARY.
(Erase heading not required.)

March 1919.

Place	Date	Hour	Summary of Events and Information	Remarks and references to Appendices
Slandr.	29th		Normal. R.E. Services only. 12 Scott received R.I.P. 8 min. Lent down to Bailleul. 10R sent to 167th Battns for H.T.O.	
Lille.	30th		Normal. 1 Escort returned but no one sent down. Instructions received but no one sent down guarding pack transit would cease on April 1st, 1919. All attached personnel would be returned to their own units & the Batalis. Cadre collected at Standré, prior to moving to Petit Aubenarde. Instructions issued to collect 60 york horses, & 10 × 3" space carts for transport for escort to 1st KOYLI at Standré pending despatch on 1st April. Demands for transport & winners made to 14th & 40th Divisions, & also, reg winnals in the way of horses & attachments sent to 16th & 74th Division. Move to Petit Aubenarde note sent for mre.	
	31st		Normal. Attached personnel collected at Standré. 3 Officers sent for demobilisation. #Lt. FLORETY. #Lt. ASHWORTH. 2nd Lt. CLARK. 8 Officers + 49 O.R. demobilized during the month. 26 Horses & 7 mules demobilized during the month. 5 O.R.'s re-enlisted during the month.	

31/3/19

Archibald Roberts, Colonel
Commanding 20th Middlesex Regt.

20th Battalion, Middlesex Regiment.

Move Orders for Army of Occupation Draft.

1. Draft for 1st Battalion, Middlesex Regiment will proceed under the Command of Lieutenant L.P. DURAND, to TOURCOING to-morrow, March 2nd to report to the R.T.O. at 01.45 hours. (Summer Time)

2. Lorries will report to the Battalion this evening, March 1st.

3. Routine for this personnel to-morrow, March 2nd will be as follows:-

If lorries available for conveyance of troops.	If lorries available only for conveyance of rations and equipment.
Reveille:- 0400.)	Reveille :- 03.30.)
Breakfast:- 0430.) Summer time.	Breakfast :- 0400.) Summer time.
Embuss:- 0515.)	March off :- 0445.)

   The Orderly Officer for March 1st will be present at the men's billets at the above times.

4. BLANKETS. will be put up by each man with his equipment. If lorries are not provided in sufficient numbers to carry the men, packs and blankets will be put on the lorries and will be available for the use of the men on the train journey.

5. Rations for consumption 2nd March will be issued to each man. Rations for consumption 3rd and 4th March will be taken in bulk.

6. If lorries are only available for equipment and rations, if possible, equipment of the two Companies ("A" and "D" Companies) should be on separate lorries and an unloading party for each Company sent on the respective lorries, a senior N.C.O. being sent in charge. This N.C.O. will, on arrival, report to the R.T.O. and arrange for the equipment to be unloaded immediately, and stacked separately by Companies.

Captain and Adjutant,
20th Battalion Middlesex Regiment.

1-3-1919.

WAR DIARY

20th Battn. Middlesex Regt.

(April 1919.)

Army Form C. 2118.

WAR DIARY
or
INTELLIGENCE SUMMARY.

(Erase heading not required.)

Instructions regarding War Diaries and Intelligence Summaries are contained in F. S. Regs., Part II. and the Staff Manual respectively. Title pages will be prepared in manuscript.

Place	Date	Hour	Summary of Events and Information	Remarks and references to Appendices

WAR DIARY
INTELLIGENCE SUMMARY

APRIL 1919.

Place	Date	Hour	Summary of Events and Information	Remarks
Standin lille	1st		Instructions issued for return of personnel of 40th Divs in 151st Div area units, on April 2nd. Personnel of York Fancs. 6 O's 40 O.R's returns 151st Div amount to-day.	
	2nd		Orders received from 43rd Brigade group HQ, that the Cadre would move to EYREGNIES on the 4th inst. As previous arrangements regarding this move to that effect that it was not urgently required to take place, had already been made with Division, this order appears anomalous. 40th Divs'n personnel returned. Detachment 5 7 O.R's of York Fancs despatches to BAISIEUX in lorries. Remainder of British detachment collected at S'andré. Orders to move on 4th cancelled. 2 O.R's sent to 29th D.L.I. for inclusion in their Cadre & 114 O.R's to 33rd Bn for onward Rpt. Cpl Hawkins sent 151st MGC forward with Regular Battn. (A/t Bn Essex. T.F.) 43rd T.M.B. demobilized.	
	3rd		2 O.R's sent to 1st By. for Army of Occupation.	
	4th		Officer A.Q. A.HICKS. (A/t Bn Essex. T.F.) 43rd T.M.B. demobilized.	
	5th		Nil	
	6th		R.C. Services in Parish Church. C/E's in the English Chapel 9 ".e.c.s.	

Army Form C. 2118.

WAR DIARY
or
INTELLIGENCE SUMMARY.
(Erase heading not required.)

April. 1919.

Place	Date	Hour	Summary of Events and Information	Remarks and references to Appendices
St Aubin	7/4		40th Divn. in Billets at WAMBRECHIES which billets between 9.00 & 10.00 hrs.	
	8/4 9/4		Warning order received that the Bn. would move to WATTRELOS on 11/4 inst.	
	9/4		Small issue of clothing available to very necessary.	
			Capt. P. BENDA MVR, Lt. S. CAREY, 2/Lt. M. E. SMITT & 2/O Sidew Robts. 3 Officers, Lt. JOHNSON, demobilised.	A.
	10/4		Preparations, orders to move to morrow. Information received from division that the transport asked for, namely 4 lorries, 17 pr & 1 sidge & horses would report at Bn H.Q. at 9.00 hrs. on 11/4.	
	11/4	9.30	2 lorries turned up. It appeared only available Officers & a proposal of Stores (loads) of Room-Demot-Officers Stores Officers Valises & ammun. Stores. Despatched at 19.50 hrs with instructions to return hess kit Cullen Stores.	
		9.45	for 2nd journey. 12 pairs of horses turned up from Divisional Train. As far as could be ascertained no more were available from the Train. Decided to leave 4 cookers & 2 water carts behind with guard of 3 men.	
		10.50	4 more pairs of horses turned up from Artillery. These took the 4 Cookers, and	

Army Form C. 2118.

WAR DIARY
or
INTELLIGENCE SUMMARY.
(Erase heading not required.)

April 1919.

Place	Date	Hour	Summary of Events and Information	Remarks and references to Appendices
Mundra	11/F		Horse, with the pair of mules already in possession, split up to take the Maltese Cart, the 15th Jun Transport less 8 water carts moved off at 11.05hr.	
		11.30hrs.	One more pair of horses arrived & took on the water carts. No more horses apparently available, so that at 13.00 hrs a pair were lent by 287 A.E.C. Company at Grandrie, so that the whole Transport was at last moved. Lorries completed 2nd Journey by 4.0p.m. Billets in WATTRELOS fairly good, & greatly improved by all the Senior NCO's being able to find separate billets themselves by this fortnight.	
WATTRELOS.	12/		Leave re-opened. Belgian Decoration Militaire (with ut Croix de Guerre) awarded to 62095 Pte J.T. GILBERT, for bravery in the action of Sept 28th 1918.	
	13/ 14/		Nil.	

WAR DIARY or INTELLIGENCE SUMMARY

Army Form C. 2118.

April 1919.

Place	Date	Hour	Summary of Events and Information	Remarks and references to Appendices
WATTRELOS	15th		3 OR's sent to 1st Battn. for Army Occupation.	
	16th		Nil.	
	17th		Bulks at HERSEAUX used from 14.00 hrs onwards.	
	18th		Nil. Information received that owing to shipping shortage, due to Colonials being returned to their own countries, it was not possible to say when details in this area would return home, but it was hoped to complete the area by July 31st.	
	19th		French MEDAILLE MILITAIRE, awarded to 58558 Pte. H. WEBBER for gallantry in action on the Scheldt in October 1918.	
	20th		Nil.	
	21st		2 Officers, 2/Lt FLEMING & 2/Lt AMBERAN sent for posts as 1st Lieut. for Army Occupation.	
	22nd			
	23rd		Nil.	
	24th		Information received that new arrangements had be made for return of cadres of this area to the Division, would probably commence going on May 16th, that is 1st, 5th & 9th notifications. Joy Rides for the men to BRUSSELS, GHENT, on May 1st. Their 2/WATTMANN demobilized received 50R per cadre for each trip. 15th	

Army Form C. 2118.

WAR DIARY
or
INTELLIGENCE SUMMARY.
(Erase heading not required.)

April 1919.

Instructions regarding War Diaries and Intelligence Summaries are contained in F. S. Regs., Part II. and the Staff Manual respectively. Title pages will be prepared in manuscript.

Place	Date	Hour	Summary of Events and Information	Remarks and references to Appendices
WATIRELOS	25th 26th 27th 28th 29th		BATS at MERSEAUX. Nil./- Information obtained, that the arrangements whereby Cadres of the Division would commence to go home about May 16th had been cancelled owing to shortage of trains, or the French said, that the thing more depends than the ought to be clear by July 31st could be stated.	
	30th		Inspection of the Demobilization Equipment by D.A.D.O.S. 7 Officers & 20 OR demobilized during the month.	

30/4/19.

O Wydeville Roberts Lt Colonel
Comdg 20th Middlesex Regt.

20th Battalion, The Middlesex Regiment.

MOVE ORDERS

10th April, 1919.

Orderly Officer tomorrow:- 2/Lieut. A.W.Bevan.
    Reveille - 07.00.
    Breakfast - 07.30.

1. Horses for Transport and 4 Lorries will report at these H.Q. at 09.00 hours tomorrow, April 11th. The Transport Sergeant will arrange for a guide to be at Orderly Room at the above time to take the horses to the Transport Lines.
The Mess and Maltese Carts will be sent round to the Officers Mess as soon as they are horsed, for Orderly Room, Demobilization and Mess stores. Packs, blankets and cooking utensils of the Transport personnel will be carried on the ½ limber at present unloaded.
Captain R.STARLING, M.C., will be in charge of the 1st Line Transport.
All Battalion Transport personnel will move with the transport.

2. LORRIES. One lorry will be sent to the Q.M.Stores. All stores personnel will travel on this lorry.
One lorry will remain at H.Q. for Officers Valises, Mess kit, etc., the Mess staff will travel on this lorry.
Two lorries will be sent down to the Billet. As much barrack furniture as possible will be carried in these lorries, besides remaining personnel. Only 50 filled palliasses will be taken. The remainder will be emptied.

3. OFFICER'S VALISES. will be stacked outside Orderly Room by 08.15.

4. LOADERS. Four men will be detailed to report to the Q.M.Stores at 09.00 hours to act as loaders. These men will probably not be able to travel on the Store Lorry.

5. MOVING OFF. 1st Line Transport will move off under the orders of Captain R.STARLING, M.C. Store lorry will move off under R.Q.M.S. A.C.CRAIG.
The two personnel lorries will be loaded under the supervision of 2/Lt. J.M.EWING. When loaded they will be brought up under the orders of this Officer to H.Q.
All other Officers must proceed to WATTRELOS by train. They will not leave until instructed by the Adjutant.

6. DESTINATION. All parties will proceed to the Square at WATTRELOS.

7. ADVANCE PARTY. 2/Lieut. C.H.MONTAGUE and 1 O.R. will proceed in advance by train under instructions already issued.

8. CLEANLINESS OF BILLETS. All billets, horse lines, etc. will be left scrupulously clean. Especial attention will be paid to Cookhouse, Latrines (these must be filled in) and incinerators. 2/Lieut. EWING will obtain a certificate from the Concierge that the Chateau has been left clean.

(Sgd) COLIN GHEE, Captain and Adjutant,
20th (S) Battalion, Middlesex Regiment.

WAR DIARY

20th Battn. Middlesex Regt.

May 1919.

Army Form C. 2118.

WAR DIARY
or
INTELLIGENCE SUMMARY.
(Erase heading not required.)

Instructions regarding War Diaries and Intelligence Summaries are contained in F. S. Regs., Part II. and the Staff Manual respectively. Title pages will be prepared in manuscript.

Place	Date	Hour	Summary of Events and Information	Remarks and references to Appendices

WAR DIARY or INTELLIGENCE SUMMARY

Army Form C. 2118.

MAY 1919

Place: WATTRELOS

Date	Hour	Summary of Events and Information
1st		LILLE, ROUBAIX, TOURCOING (+ Tagetroels) public houses to-day, in view of French strikes + political meetings.
2nd		Balks at Herseaux. Higher authority ask "why the detachment at St André has not yet been withdrawn." 10 OR's realistic. Demobilizes.
3rd		nil
4th		
5th		
6th		nil
7th		
8th		
9th		Orders to reduce Cadre by 10 O.R's. is 1st establishment of 36 O.R's including OR Sergeant after having already been demobilized without any reference to this Cadre 35 O.R's after Base. latter having already been demobilized without any reference to this Cadre. Latter having decided that it would be permissible to make establishment of the Cadre having been admitted to Hospital + Struck owing to 10R on the strength of the Cadre was really retainable. Though records off strength + the discovery that another OR on the Cadre was previously shown him as available for demobilization as being order 37 (C being born in 1896) only 8 O.R's could be sent for demobilizations. 10R posted to 12th Middlesex.

Officer, $\frac{Lt}{t}$ A.E. STABLER, demobilizes from OWN HQ.

Army Form C. 2118.

WAR DIARY
or
INTELLIGENCE SUMMARY.
(Erase heading not required.)

MAY 1919

Instructions regarding War Diaries and Intelligence Summaries are contained in F. S. Regs., Part II. and the Staff Manual respectively. Title pages will be prepared in manuscript.

Place	Date	Hour	Summary of Events and Information	Remarks and references to Appendices
WATRELOS	10th		Nil	
	11th			
	12th		9 ORs. Returnable for Army S/occupatn., others 516 Batty from xr Corps H.C.r.S. Camp at Tournai.	
	13th		Scend Brussels Trip — only 3 ORs proceeded. Major G.H.SCRIVEN posted to 69 P/w Company, to take command H.Q. MURRAY posted to 379 P/w Company. this disposes of Remaining officer volunteers for Service with army S/occupatn. 9 ORs. despatched to 13th Middlesex Regt for A.S/O.	
	14th			
	15th		Nil	
	16th			
	17th		Information received from Major G.H.SCRIVEN, at ROUEN, where 69 P/w Company was reported to be, on the instructions received opening his posting, that he had just discovered that the Company was at MOUSCRON - about half an hours walk from Wattrelos!	
	18th		Nil	

Army Form C. 2118.

WAR DIARY
or
INTELLIGENCE SUMMARY.
(Erase heading not required.)

MAY 1919

Instructions regarding War Diaries and Intelligence Summaries are contained in F. S. Regs., Part II. and the Staff Manual respectively. Title pages will be prepared in manuscript.

Place	Date	Hour	Summary of Events and Information	Remarks and references to Appendices
WATERLOO	19/15		1 OR demobilized.	
	20/15, 21/15		nil.	
	22/15		2 OR posted to 13th Battn for Army of Occupation. Third Brussels trip. CO's proceeded.	
	24/15, 25/15		nil	
	26/15		Instructions received that Cadres would probably be reduced to CO, 2nd in command, 16 NCO's, as personnel for loading at Railheads & Ports would be specially provided.	
	27/15, 28/15		nil	
	29/15		Instructions received on 26th Cancelled. Reduction by 75% of original Cadre establishment substituted. Makes Cadre strength to be about 12 OR's, but numbers of officers not known exactly. No action to be taken at present. 1 Officer Capt. B. P. Good, sent for dispersal	

Army Form C. 2118.

WAR DIARY
or
INTELLIGENCE SUMMARY.
(Erase heading not required.)

MAY 1919

Place	Date	Hour	Summary of Events and Information	Remarks and references to Appendices
WAITRELOS	30		Request from French Mission to make the Oak Stocks, required for the "Comité de Secours" already housed in the local School, but a sudden desire to inculcate knowledge in the minds of the young Whi nation, has forced the Comité to evacuate the seat of learning. Several alternative places were shown by the local Gendarme, but they were mostly too many miles away from the nearest restaurant to satisfy the task of the Quartermaster. Finally an estaminet, unused as such, but with lace curtains to windows on the mantelpiece, selected as being most suitable.	
	31st		The work of moving a complete Regimental stock of equipment 200 yards with the assistance of two 2 mules commenced. 20 Officers & 10 ORs demobilized during the month.	

Ch Tun
Capt.
20th Bn Middlesex Cadr.

WAR DIARY.

20th Batt. Middlesex Regt.

1st – 18th June 1919

WO 37
Covered

Army Form C. 2118.

WAR DIARY
or
INTELLIGENCE SUMMARY.

(Erase heading not required.)

Instructions regarding War Diaries and Intelligence Summaries are contained in F. S. Regs., Part II. and the Staff Manual respectively. Title pages will be prepared in manuscript.

Place	Date	Hour	Summary of Events and Information	Remarks and references to Appendices

(A7092). Wt. W1869/M1292. 750,000. 1/17. D. D & L., Ltd. Forms/C2118/14.

Army Form C. 2118.

WAR DIARY
or
INTELLIGENCE SUMMARY.
(Erase heading not required).

JUNE 1919

Place	Date	Hour	Summary of Events and Information	Remarks and references to Appendices
WAITREUX	1st		nil	
	2nd		Orders received that 'Cadre' would proceed to Maudri Demobilization Camp on June 14th. Equipment Guard to consist of 2 officers & 12 O.R's to be collected at Petit Audenarde on June 12th. Equipment Guard selected	
	3rd		nil	
	4th		Extract from King's Birthday Honours despatch June 1919. Distinguished Service Order. 1st R.C.E.M. Richards. M.C. Distinguished Conduct Medal. 158412 Sgt. T.R.H. Truss. 140145 Sgt. F. Lee. Instructions received with	
	5th		a few alterations in Equipment Guard made. Regard to disposal of a.3rd T.M.B stores on 18th inst.	
	6th		Instructions received regarding move to Petit Audenarde. Accommodation there. Also permission to despatch Organisation of Equipment Guards after June 12th. Cadre to start but on 12th inst.	
	7th		Orders that Commanding Officer must proceed with Cadres to Base Ports. Wonderful & complicated instructions received regarding packing, sealing, numbering & cataloguing all packages, vehicles & other stores.	

Army Form C. 2118.

WAR DIARY
or
INTELLIGENCE SUMMARY.
(Erase heading not required.)

JUNE 1919

Place	Date	Hour	Summary of Events and Information	Remarks and references to Appendices
WATTRELOS	8th 9th 10th 11th		Final arrangements regarding move on 12th. Ets. Leave arrangements completed. Leave arrangements for all personnel on leave to join immediately. Period for all personnel on leave to join immediately. Moved to Petit Audenarde - Equipment guard to St Audré ↓ Cadr. Pen ↓	
	12th		Move to Petit Audenarde. Equipment guard arrived 8.30 am - ½ hour early. 16 Pairs of Horses arrived 9.00 am Lorry for Cadr arrived 8.30 am - ½ hour early. 16 Pairs of Horses also ½ hour early. What view of the Cadre Party could be found from the local established to transhandle the wagons into position for harnessing up. Quartermaster & Transport Sergeant. 1st load of wagons got off by 10.30 hrs. Quartermaster & Transport Sergeant proceeded with them to supervise parking at Petit Audenarde. 2nd load of wagons at 11.30 hrs. Cadre got off at 10.45 hrs. 2nd load of wagons & lt Stradia - a great feat! all wagons parked in yard of new O.M. Stores & lt Stradia - a great feat! else mess Cart had to be sent back to wattrelos in the afternoon for kits etc. of men on leave. Orders received in the afternoon that Equipment guard would entrain at HERSEAUX Station on 13th inst. Destination in England to take his wife home from TOURCOING. Thought officer and now 1 CSM, 1 Sgt, 1 Cpl his wife home from TOURCOING. Thought officer and now 1 CSM, 1 Sgt, 1 Cpl & 12 ORS instead of 1 Offr & 4 instead of 1 Offr & 12 ORS.	

Army Form C. 2118.

WAR DIARY
or
INTELLIGENCE SUMMARY.
(Erase heading not required.)

JUNE 1919.

Place	Date	Hour	Summary of Events and Information	Remarks and references to Appendices
PETIT AUDENARDE	13th		Clearing up documents, surplus stores. Indenting for of stores etc. Surplus taken into Base Cash'ier Lille. (No closed. 1 OR returned off leave. Detailed orders re going into training received.	
	14th		Commanding Officer to St Amise Demobilization Camp to take Command of Cadre Party. Supres Account of Lille closed. Sorting of documents for records etc. Cleaning up, packing T/6.	
	15th		Finishing up: all documents for Records ready for despatch. 3 OR's returned off leave. Completing demobilization. Papers of equipment guard.	
	16th		Documents for preservation despatched to Records. 43rd T.M.B. Stores (reserve) taken over. 3 wor OR's returned from leave. Strength of equipment guard was all but short. Orders received that 4 pairs of horses would work for this unit to-morrow afternoon, instead of 2 prs up to morning of 18th	
	17th		T.M.B. Stores handed over. Area stores concentrated in Q.M. Stores. All wagons except 2 moved up to HERSEAUX Station to await movement. Rest of equipment A.K. at last queen — CHIMEL. This being cleaned by fitters. Equipment of allocated for all wagons.	

Army Form C. 2118.

WAR DIARY
or
INTELLIGENCE SUMMARY.   JUNE 1919.
(Erase heading not required.)

Instructions regarding War Diaries and Intelligence Summaries are contained in F. S. Regs., Part II. and the Staff Manual respectively. Title pages will be prepared in manuscript.

Place	Date	Hour	Summary of Events and Information	Remarks and references to Appendices
PETIT MOURMELON	18		Train comes in at 7.00 h.s. & checked down & roped by 2.0 p.m. Train leaves punctually at 9.0 p.m. Bosche arrives 9.30 h.s. All wagons loaded & thus ends la grande guerre.	

FINIS

Chas Lacey Capt
8C
20th Middlesex R⁺

www.ingramcontent.com/pod-product-compliance
Lightning Source LLC
Chambersburg PA
CBHW080915230426
43667CB00015B/2684